HOW TO OPEN & OPERATE
A FINANCIALLY SUCCESSFUL

WEB-BASED

BUSINESS

WITH COMPANION CD-ROM

BY BETH WILLIAMS

HOW TO OPEN & OPERATE A FINANCIALLY SUCCESSFUL WEB-BASED BUSINESS — WITH COMPANION CD-ROM

Copyright © 2007 by Atlantic Publishing Group, Inc.
1405 SW 6th Ave. • Ocala, Florida 34471 • 800-814-1132 • 352-622-1875–Fax
Web site: www.atlantic-pub.com • E-mail: sales@atlantic-pub.com
SAN Number: 268-1250

ISBN-13: 978-1-60138-118-7   ISBN-10: 1-60138-118-2

Library of Congress Cataloging-in-Publication Data

Williams, Beth, 1973-
   How to open & operate a financially successful web-based business : with companion CD-ROM / by Beth Williams.
      p. cm.
   Includes bibliographical references and index.
   ISBN-13: 978-1-60138-118-7 (alk. paper)
   ISBN-10: 1-60138-118-2 (alk. paper)
   1. Electronic commerce. 2. Internet marketing. 3. New business enterprises--Management. I. Title. II. Title: How to open and operate a financially successful web-based business.

   HF5548.32.W545 2007
   658.8'72--dc22
                                    2007025039

Printed on Recycled Paper

EDITOR: Tracie Kendziora • tkendziora@atlantic-pub.com
PROOFREADER: Vickie Taylor • vtaylor@atlantic-pub.com

Printed in the United States

We recently lost our beloved pet "Bear," who was not only our best and dearest friend but also the "Vice President of Sunshine" here at Atlantic Publishing. He did not receive a salary but worked tirelessly 24 hours a day to please his parents. Bear was a rescue dog that turned around and showered myself, my wife Sherri, his grandparents Jean, Bob and Nancy and every person and animal he met (maybe not rabbits) with friendship and love. He made a lot of people smile every day.

We wanted you to know that a portion of the profits of this book will be donated to The Humane Society of the United States.

–Douglas & Sherri Brown

THE HUMANE SOCIETY
OF THE UNITED STATES ©

The human-animal bond is as old as human history. We cherish our animal companions for their unconditional affection and acceptance. We feel a thrill when we glimpse wild creatures in their natural habitat or in our own backyard.

Unfortunately, the human-animal bond has at times been weakened. Humans have exploited some animal species to the point of extinction.

The Humane Society of the United States makes a difference in the lives of animals here at home and worldwide. The HSUS is dedicated to creating a world where our relationship with animals is guided by compassion. We seek a truly humane society in which animals are respected for their intrinsic value, and where the human-animal bond is strong.

Want to help animals? We have plenty of suggestions. Adopt a pet from a local shelter, join The Humane Society and be a part of our work to help companion animals and wildlife. You will be funding our educational, legislative, investigative and outreach projects in the U.S. and across the globe.

Or perhaps you'd like to make a memorial donation in honor of a pet, friend or relative? You can through our Kindred Spirits program. And if you'd like to contribute in a more structured way, our Planned Giving Office has suggestions about estate planning, annuities, and even gifts of stock that avoid capital gains taxes.

Maybe you have land that you would like to preserve as a lasting habitat for wildlife. Our Wildlife Land Trust can help you. Perhaps the land you want to share is a backyard—that's enough. Our Urban Wildlife Sanctuary Program will show you how to create a habitat for your wild neighbors.

So you see, it's easy to help animals. And The HSUS is here to help.

The Humane Society of the United States
2100 L Street NW
Washington, DC 20037
202-452-1100
www.hsus.org

CONTENTS

FOREWORD

By Bruce C. Brown

A 2006 Forrester Research study of 174 retailers found that online retail sales rose last year by 25 percent, to $176.4 billion, and are expected to rise 20 percent in 2006, to $211.4 billion. By 2010, sales should reach $329 billion. The potential for realizing success through a Web-based business is realistic and attainable. Nothing is more invigorating, exciting, and empowering than owning your own business. By harnessing the power of the Internet and establishing your own Web presence, you can own and operate a Web-based business within the comfortable confines of your home office. While owning a Web-based business can be rewarding and satisfying, it also can be a monumental failure if you have not carefully charted out your playbook for success.

I have owned my own Web design and computer support company for the past ten years and have had my share of successes and failures. Unfortunately, I did not have an all-inclusive, fact-filled guide which walked me through the process to ensure I had a viable business plan, financial backing, and the industry knowledge to succeed. This is where *How to Open & Operate a Financially Successful Web-Based Business (With Companion CD-ROM)* by Beth Williams comes into play. Best intentions, great ideas, and hard work are often not enough to establish a successful online business — it takes planning, strategy, marketing, and versatility. This book provides a complete and thorough guide through every stage of creating a Web-based business, from developing business and marketing plans to designing your Web site and achieving high rankings in popular search engines.

In my ten years as a Web-based business owner, I have never come across a compilation of information as useful as that in this book. This book covers every single aspect of developing a successful Web-based business and provides you with a wealth of information, ideas, and action plans. It covers topics such as how to price your products and services, how to maintain legal compliance, how to find your market niche, type of businesses, business licenses, taxes, Web site design, Web site hosting, search engine marketing, e-commerce, and provides you with a wealth of innovative ideas to increase revenue and helps ensure the profitability and stability of your Web-based business.

There are literally dozens of books on the market about how to start your own business which offer conflicting, difficult to follow, or outdated information, as well as Internet-based, get rich quick schemes, which always result in failure. *How to Open &Operate a Financially Successful Web-Based Business* sets itself apart as the best resource available for how to start a successful Web-based business. This book is not about get rich quick schemes; instead, it is a methodically documented resource guide to help you achieve success and covers all the critical facets of planning and establishing a Web-based business. It is well written, easy to read, and provides you with the right amount of detail. It will inevitably be an invaluable desk reference you will rely on heavily and frequently. While the book is chock full of vital information, it is also written for the beginner, not the seasoned Web professional. You do not need to have an MBA or be a professional Web site designer to understand and implement the ideas, business plans, and strategies outlined in this book. I am so impressed with the quality and quantity of information contained in this book and the pragmatic, straight to the point writing style that I would recommend this book be required reading for anyone contemplating a Web-based business. This book will be a trusty business partner, which you will read and use often.

Bruce C. Brown is the best selling author of How to Use the Internet to Advertise, Promote and Market Your Business or Web Site with Little or No Money *and recently completed his third book entitled* The Ultimate Guide to Search Engine Marketing: Pay Per Click Advertising Secrets Revealed. *Bruce is finishing his 23rd year as an officer in the United States Coast Guard and is looking forward to retirement when he can concentrate on helping others succeed with their online businesses and marketing campaigns. He uses his 20+ years of expertise in financial management in conjunction with more than 12 years as a web designer, business owner, e-marketing consultant, and hardware and software specialist. He completed college during his military career, earning degrees from the University of Phoenix and Charter Oak State College. He currently splits his time between Washington, DC and Land O Lakes, Florida, with his wife, Vonda, and youngest son, Colton. His oldest son, Dalton, is a full-time student at the University of South Florida in Tampa (Go Bulls!), and his middle son, Jordan, is a full-time student at the University of Florida in Gainesville (Go Gators!).*

SHOULD YOU START YOUR OWN WEB-BASED BUSINESS?

M any people dream of starting their own business, and because of the convenience, ease, and popularity of the Internet, an increasing amount of would-be entrepreneurs are tossing their hats in the ring and starting Web-based businesses.

One of the biggest selling points of a Web-based business is the fact that startup costs are minimal. Technically, all you really need to start a Web-based business is a computer, a reliable Internet connection, a Web site, and a good idea. Of course, it also takes a lot of hard work, but minimal equipment and money are needed to start.

Additionally, whereas you can reach only a certain segment of the population with a traditional brick and mortar business, a Web-based business has the potential to reach millions of customers around the globe, provided you offer a product or a service that is in demand but that is not in a market already saturated with similar businesses.

A HOT COMMODITY: SHOPPING ONLINE

There can be little doubt that the Internet makes our collective lives easier, from allowing us to pay our bills online to making it easy and convenient to purchase gifts and other necessities. The number of people spending online has been consistently increasing, resulting in consumers spending billions of dollars online per quarter.

According to the United States Department of Commerce, "The estimate of U.S. retail e-commerce sales for the second quarter of 2006, adjusted for seasonal variation and holiday and trading-day differences, but not for price changes, was $26.3 billion, an increase of 4.6 percent (±1.7%) from the first quarter of 2006. Total retail sales for the second quarter of 2006 were estimated at $984.9 billion, an increase of 0.9 percent (±0.3%) from the first quarter of 2006."

As more people turn to the Internet for their retail needs, more entrepreneurs are realizing the rich opportunities a Web-based business can offer. But to ensure the success of a Web-based business, one must understand the storied history of online businesses and learn from the mistakes of those entrepreneurs who reveled in and ultimately failed in the dotcom boom.

WEB-BASED BUSINESSES – A BRIEF HISTORY

Web-based businesses saw their greatest surge in the early 1990s with the dotcom boom. At the height of the dotcom boom, venture capital firms in Silicon Valley in California – the heart of the boom – were pulling in an estimated two billion dollars per week.

Entrepreneurs saw a golden opportunity and took their chances. Dotcoms sprang up all over the Internet, and entrepreneurs saw dollar signs. One reason for the demise of many dotcoms in the late '90s was an imbalance between the individual dotcom's spending and actual profits. Many entrepreneurs spent far more than they were actually making – hiring employees and paying extremely high wages, even to those employees on the low rung of the company ladder; paying for luxurious offices; and expending huge amounts of money on advertising their product or service. Ultimately, many of these Web-based businesses went bust as a result of their expenditures far outweighing their profits.

Another reason for some of the biggest failures of Web-based businesses during the dotcom boom was the fact that many of these businesses did not have sustainable ideas. An example is the technology magazine CNET named Webvan, an online credit and delivery grocery business. It was the biggest flop of the dotcom boom, a distinction no company wants to hold.

The idea behind Webvan, founded in 1999, was simple. Customers could go online and place their grocery orders, which would then be delivered to them. The company raised a stunning $375 million in capital in a year and a half. Webvan began operations in San Francisco, California, and eventually expanded to eight cities (Chicago, Los Angeles, Orange County, Portland, San Diego, San Francisco, and Seattle), with major plans to add offices in more than 26 cities in the United States. Webvan had high hopes, including numerous high-tech warehouses that were on order for $1 billion. At the height of their success, Webvan was worth more than one billion dollars with shares peaking at $30 per share.

Unfortunately, the online grocery market was not as big as Webvan had hoped. In fact, financial experts point to a simple error in judgment: Just because consumers have unpleasant experiences offline (such as waiting in long lines at the grocery store) does not mean they will automatically turn to the Internet to fulfill their needs. In fact, according to a Jupiter Media Matrix study cited in Wired News, only two percent of all consumers in 2000 (a year before Webvan went bust) turned to online grocers for their grocery needs.

Webvan expanded in leaps and bounds, but their customer base remained stagnant. Webvan's downfall began as early as 2001, when they lost a stunning $217 million in the first quarter and had amassed a debt of more than $800 million.

In the end, Webvan was forced to declare bankruptcy, permanently shutting down operations in July 2001. Ultimately, more than 2,000 employees lost their jobs.

Webvan was not, however, the only dotcom to go under as the dotcom bust of the late 1990s took hold.

Today, some are questioning if the dotcom bust was really as dire as many originally believed. In fact, a study conducted by researchers at the University of Maryland's Robert H. Smith School of Business and the University of California at San Diego found that of the more than 700 Web-based businesses that requested venture capital funds in the 1990s, 45 percent of those businesses survived for at least five years. Among those companies that were born as a result of the dotcom boom, and are now multi-million dollar companies, are Amazon, Netscape, Yahoo, and eBay.

But whether or not the bust of the dotcom boom in the late 1990s was as expansive as originally believed, there are plenty of lessons to be learned about what to do and what not to do when you start your Web-based business. First, if you want to succeed with your Web-based business, you must find your niche (which we will talk about in-depth in Chapter Two). The idea behind Webvan may have been revolutionary, but the company simply did not have a large enough target market to make the business a success.

Second, do not try to put your Web-based business on the fast track to growth. It takes time to grow a business. Again, Webvan is an excellent example of this concept. The company poured so much money into expanding the business that they failed to recognize that the market for an online grocer just was not there.

Despite the dotcom boom and subsequent bust, entrepreneurs have been building Web-based businesses for years. And there is even an inkling that a new dotcom boom is in the infant stages. Such iconic media outlets as the New York Times and the British Broadcasting Corporation (BBC) are hinting that Google's purchase of YouTube, for $1.65 billion, could be the signal that dotcoms are about to boom again.

Google, by no means, is the first to make such a monumental acquisition. In fact, eBay purchased voice and instant messenger Skype for $2.65 billion, while the virtual meeting place MySpace was purchased by News Corporation, owned by media mogul Rupert Murdoch, for $580 million.

Experts point out that a second dotcom boom has much more potential for being successful because of what has been learned from the first boom. For instance, today's Web-based business owners realize that the key to really making money online is through advertising.

Regardless of what has happened with Web-based businesses in the past, these businesses are the wave of the future because of the convenience and ease they offer consumers. With that in mind, there are also a plethora of benefits of starting your own Web-based business.

THE BENEFITS OF STARTING A WEB-BASED BUSINESS

There is nothing more powerful than the opportunity to seize control of your life, your career, and your future by running your own Web-based business. But there are also those smaller benefits that you will really appreciate as an entrepreneur:

- You can work from home.

- You will likely have low startup costs.

- Until your Web-based business starts making a profit, you can keep your day job and work on your business in the evenings and on weekends.

- You do not have to worry about the expense of renting office or retail space.

- You will likely have low operating costs, which means you will be able to keep more of your profits.

- Once you start working with your Web-based business full-time, you will no longer have to worry about sitting in bumper-to-bumper traffic every morning and every evening. Getting to your office will likely take only a few steps.

- You can ditch the suit or uncomfortable heels. Working from home means you can dress how you want.

- You are your own boss, so you run your business how you want.

- You can work when you want.

- You can let your creativity run free.

- You will enjoy a variety of tax advantages as a self-employed business owner.

- You no longer have to worry about stressful office gossip and office politics.

- Your business will be open 24/7, allowing customers to purchase your products (if you are selling products) even when you are asleep or enjoying time off.

In addition to these benefits, there are a few downsides of which you should at least be aware. If your office is in your home, you are going to want to consider setting office hours, especially if you are surrounded by temptations like TV, playing with your kids, or helping your spouse with chores.

Setting concrete office hours will allow you and your family to establish boundaries as to when you are available and when you must focus on your work. It is easy to get sidetracked when you work from home, so you will need to learn to discipline yourself.

Another potential downside is you are going to be working for yourself and by yourself. Therefore, you are going to be isolated, and your immediate support system is going to be limited. Your family and loved ones will be able to offer support, but you also need to find other entrepreneurs who understand what you are going through and with whom you can share mutual support. This is one reason it is incredibly important that you network — something we will discuss later in this book.

As an entrepreneur, you are also going to be solely responsible for your Web-based business's success, which may be considered an advantage or a disadvantage depending on your viewpoint.

Now that you know the advantages and disadvantages of starting your own Web-based business, you probably know if this is the path you want to pursue. In the next section, we will discuss the important characteristics of successful entrepreneurs.

DO YOU HAVE WHAT IT TAKES TO RUN YOUR OWN WEB-BASED BUSINESS?

Entrepreneurs are a different breed: They are focused, determined, and not afraid of hard work. Because starting a Web-based business — or any business, for that matter — takes hard work and dedication, you should take the time to assess why you want to start your own Web-based business and whether you possess the traits that are commonly found in successful entrepreneurs. Keep in mind, however, that you can work to acquire or to hone many of these traits if you set your mind to it.

To start, you must ask yourself why you want to start your own Web-based business. Ask yourself:

- Do you want to be your own boss?

- Are you bored with having a traditional nine to five job?

- Do you want the opportunity to do what you want when you want and how you want?

- Do you hope to improve your standard of living?

- Do you believe the product or service you have to offer fills a need in the marketplace?

- Are you seeking a challenge?

- Do you want to take control of your career and your life?

The idea of starting one's own business sounds almost romantic. You get to be your own boss; you can work from home — even in your pajamas, if you want — and you have full control of exactly how your business is run. It sounds like a dream, and for many people, unfortunately, it remains just that.

Realistically, running your own Web-based business is going to take hard work. Keep in mind that there is no guarantee that your Web-based business is going to succeed or make money in the early days. In fact, the Small Business Administration states, "Over 50 percent of small businesses fail in the first year and 95 percent fail within the first five years."

Starting a business — online or off — is by no means easy. Are you ready for the challenge? Before you give up your day job, make sure you really take what you learn in this chapter into consideration. Start by answering the following questions to assess whether you have the characteristics commonly found in successful entrepreneurs.

Do you have the time? Starting and running a business takes significant time, especially in the beginning. If you work full-time, do you have the energy to work on your Web-based business at night and on weekends? Are you willing to sacrifice your social life in the short-term for the potential benefits of a successful business in the long-term?

What about your personal life? Are you willing to sacrifice the time you generally spend with family and loved ones to concentrate on your Web-based business? Remember, you are going to be putting a lot of time and effort into starting your business, which means your family will not get as much of your time: Are you and your family willing to make that sacrifice?

Are you patient? Your Web-based business may not make money for the first six months to a year, perhaps even longer. Are you patient and determined enough to work until your Web-based business starts making a profit? Because you may not make a profit in the beginning, you will want to make sure you have sufficient funds to sustain you for a minimum of six months if you decide to forgo your day job to focus on your Web-based business full-time.

Do you have space to work? In all likelihood, you are going to be starting your Web-based business from home. Do you have sufficient space for your office? You may be able to convert a spare bedroom or a corner of your den into an office, but keep in mind that to achieve maximum productivity, you should keep your office space separate from your living space.

Are you a self-starter? Entrepreneurs do not have anyone standing over them, tapping on their shoulders to remind them that a deadline is looming. Successful entrepreneurs are self-starters who know how to get the job done and get it done right. You must have the discipline to plan, organize, and run your business.

Are you driven? Starting and running a business can often feel like a roller coaster ride: You will likely be challenged like never before, and you will be responsible for the business. Are you motivated enough to push forward when obstacles stand in your way? You must realize and accept that there will be times when you are going to experience burnout, and being driven will help you through such difficult periods.

Are you a leader? Entrepreneurs are leaders, not followers. You must have confidence in your abilities. Your Web-based business may grow to a point where you need employees or independent contractors, in which case your role as leader will be imperative.

Are you competitive? Business is highly competitive: Do you thrive on competition, or does it stress you out?

Are you a decision maker? You are your business, and you are going to have to make all of the decisions, sometimes very quickly and under stressful circumstances.

Are you good at organization and planning? Planning is vital to a business's success. According to the Small Business Administration, one of the major reasons small businesses fail is due to a lack of planning and organization.

Are you customer-oriented? A key ingredient to Web-based business success is customer service. Are you the type of person who will do whatever it takes to keep your customers happy and to gain new customers?

Take the time to really think about and answer the preceding questions. Above all, be honest with yourself. If you do not think you have what it takes to start a Web-based business now, start working on the traits that you are lacking and start when you are ready.

KEYS TO SUCCESS

As noted previously, the Small Business Administration estimates that half of all new businesses fail because of poor planning. In addition to having the traits that it takes to succeed, you must:

- Write a strong business plan; tweak it as your business grows and follow it. Remember that old cliché — if you fail to plan, you plan to fail.

- Find a niche that is in demand, but make sure the marketplace is not already saturated with products or services to fill that demand.

- Offer a product or service that is unique from that of your competitors.

- Create a strong marketing and advertising plan, and follow through with it.

- Ensure your Web site has strong, attention-grabbing content and looks professional.

- Offer top-notch customer service to your customers.

TYPES OF WEB-BASED BUSINESSES

Just as there are different types of brick and mortar businesses, there are several types of Web-based businesses that you will want to consider and understand before determining which path, or paths, you want to take. The opportunities for success online are endless, if you are willing to work hard.

Take Your Existing Brick and Mortar Business Online

If you already have an offline business, you may want to consider bringing it online to complement your offline sales. In today's high tech world, a business without a Web site is behind the times and is certainly putting itself at a disadvantage. Many customers want at least the choice of being able to purchase products online, and having an online presence offers your customers that very choice.

There are several distinct advantages to expanding your business to the Internet. In addition to literally reaching a worldwide market, you are going to make your customers' lives much easier by giving them the option of purchasing what they need from you online at any time of the day or the night.

Other advantages to taking your brick and mortar business online include:

- With a professional Web site, you can easily compete with Fortune 500 companies. A professional Web site makes you look like a million bucks, even though you may not be worth it just yet.

- You can advertise to clients on your Web site, helping curb your costs for print advertisements.

- An effective Web site will help you create brand recognition on the Internet.

- You can offer even more effective customer service. Many businesses offer customer support online by way of e-mail and/or live chat.

To determine whether your business has the potential to thrive online, ask yourself the following questions:

- Does your product appeal to a widespread customer base or is it a product that appeals to only a select, local audience?

- Do you have a product that can easily be delivered to your customers?

- Does your product allow for affordable shipping to your customers?

- Can you affordably bring customers to your Web site?

There are many advantages to bringing your brick and mortar business online, as mentioned above. If you feel your business is simply not conducive to the Internet, however, you may want to consider starting a Web-based business from scratch.

Startup

Starting a Web-based business from the ground up is the avenue many entrepreneurs choose to pursue. If you are going to start a Web-based business from scratch, you need a product or a service to offer your customers.

There are thousands of Web-based businesses that offer all types of products, ranging from home-baked cookies and gift baskets to handcrafted furniture and handmade knick knacks. The possibilities are literally endless and are limited only by your imagination.

Your Web-based business does not necessarily have to offer a product. You could also offer professional services, such as writing, editing, proofreading, Web design, graphic design, Internet marketing, administrative support (transcription, word processing, data entry, etc.), consulting, tutoring, and legal advice (if you are an attorney). Of course, this is only a partial listing of the services you could offer with a Web-based business. There are literally hundreds of professional services that can be and are sold through Web-based businesses. If you have a talent or a skill that other people need, you have a potential business.

The prime difference between offering a product and a service is you can physically deliver the product to your customer quickly while a service — such as writing or Web design — can take time, and there is nothing tangible to give to your customer until the project is underway.

If you are going to be selling your service, you have to approach your business in a slightly different way than you would if you were selling a product. Sometimes selling a service is more difficult, in that customers do not always want to pay for a product upfront if they do not know you or if they have not worked with you before. There are several ways you can alleviate your customers' concern.

First, you can offer them testimonials from previous satisfied customers. In addition to putting testimonials on your Web site, offer potential customers the e-mail addresses or phone numbers of several previous clients who have given their permission for potential customers to call them.

After you finish a project for a client, ask that client for a written testimonial, which you can then place on your Web site. Eventually, you will have a long list of testimonials and may want to put only the best testimonials on your Web site.

Second, make sure your credentials are listed clearly on your Web site. If you are a Web designer, list your credentials, including education and experience. An online portfolio is also an excellent marketing tool that will allow your prospective clients to see your previous work.

However, make sure you own the copyright to the material in your portfolio. For example, if you are a writer, you may have been hired by a client to ghostwrite a series of articles, and you agreed to transfer all copyrights to the client upon completion of and payment for the articles. In such a case, you would be forbidden to use those articles in your portfolio unless the client gives you permission to do so. (You may want to get the permission in writing, so you have physical evidence that you were allowed to use the articles.)

Third, many service-based businesses require customers to pay 50 percent of the project cost at the beginning of the project and 50 percent upon completion. You might also want to consider using a Statement of Work. A Statement of Work is a document in which you will outline the exact services you will provide for the customer, including project milestones and final cost.

Regardless of whether you sell a product or a service, you will have to determine how you will accept payments from customers. You may accept PayPal (**www.paypal.com**), Google Checkout (**www.checkout.google. com**), or 2Checkout (**www.2Checkout.com**). We will discuss payment methods more in-depth in Chapter 12, "Merchant Accounts and Customer Payment Options."

Affiliate-Based Online Business

If you are at all Internet savvy, you have likely already heard of affiliates or you may already be an affiliate. If you have not heard of affiliate marketing, do not worry; it is a simple concept to understand. You find products online that you want to promote, and for each sale that is made through your Web site or your affiliate ID, you are given a commission.

Affiliates can make anywhere from 10 to 50 percent of each sale, and you will generally get paid your commission twice a month from a company like ClickBank. ClickBank is a popular Web site that brings together buyers, sellers, and affiliates. When you sign up with ClickBank, you are issued an affiliate ID.

You will use your affiliate ID as a link on your Web site. When a Web site visitor clicks on that link and purchases a product you are promoting, you earn a commission. Your commission is tracked by the affiliate ID — either the person (whose product you are promoting) tracks your sales, or a middleman like ClickBank tracks sales for both of you.

Affiliate-based online businesses are incredibly popular because of how easy it is to get started. In fact, with most affiliate programs, it is free for you to sign up. However, there are downsides to affiliate marketing. First, you will not be the only one promoting a product, and in some cases, you may be competing with hundreds or thousands of other affiliates, making it a challenge to draw consumers to your particular Web site.

Second, you are not guaranteed an income from affiliate marketing, which is true of any Web-based business. But make no mistake about it: There are those affiliates — known as super affiliates — who make a substantial amount of money with their affiliate-based businesses.

However, the good news is that not all affiliates actively promote the product or products they are trying to sell. In fact, according to New Era Ventures LLC, approximately five to ten percent of affiliates actually promote products.

To actively promote products, which we will discuss further in Chapter 11, "Marketing Your Web-Based Business," you can use a variety of methods, including an e-newsletter, banner links on your Web site, banner links on other Web sites, and pay-per-click Google, Yahoo, or MSN ads.

Keep in mind that if you decide to advertise via e-newsletter or e-mail that you cannot just send out mass e-mails promoting your product. You must offer your Web site visitors the opportunity to opt-in to your e-mail or e-newsletter list. Spam is a huge problem online. You likely get dozens, if not hundreds, of spam messages in your e-mail inbox on a weekly basis, especially if you have a free e-mail provider such as Yahoo or Hotmail. The bottom line is: You do NOT want to be caught sending out spam. We will discuss spam and the consequences of sending it in the next chapter.

You might want to start a content-rich Web site that pertains to the product or products you are promoting. For example, you may be an affiliate for several popular dog food products. You want to draw customers to your Web site by offering them more than affiliate links to the products you are promoting.

You want to give them something valuable for the time they spend on your Web site. We will discuss this in later chapters, but here is a quick overview: Strong, keyword rich content is essential to draw traffic to your Web site. If you are promoting dog food products, you may want to have articles on your Web site that deal with dog health. For example, "The Best Diet for Your Puppy" or "How Your Dog's Diet Should Change As He Ages."

Ensure that each article has valuable information in it that will compel visitors to click on your affiliate link. We will discuss how to write fresh, attention-grabbing content in Chapter 10, "Creating Powerful Content for Your Web Site."

If you are an **Amazon.com** affiliate, as another example, you might advertise Amazon products by way of a Web site that reviews books, CDs, DVDs, and other merchandise found on Amazon. Each time someone purchases a product from your Web site, you will receive a commission from Amazon.

As mentioned earlier, starting a Web-based affiliate business is actually very easy. Virtually anyone can be an affiliate, but it will take work if you want to make a significant amount of money.

You can start by searching for products, in your niche, that you would like to promote.

You might want to visit ClickBank at **www.clickbank.com** or Commission Junction at **www.cj.com**. Both offer thousands of products you can check out, and most products offer affiliate programs. Signing up for ClickBank and Commission Junction is easy.

You can also visit the Web sites of some of your favorite products to see if the manufacturer has an affiliate program. Most major companies, such as Sony and Amazon, do have their own affiliate programs.

The most important decision you are going to have to make is what product or products you want to promote. Start by finding a product that is sold by a reputable company. Conduct online research to find out what other people are saying about the company. You might also want to find out whether the company is listed with the Better Business Bureau (**www.bbb. org**) and, if so, whether there are complaints against the company.

You also want to look for a product that offers a substantial commission for each sale. Why promote a product with a 5 percent commission when you can be earning a 25 to 75 percent commission on other products?

One of your keys to success as an affiliate is making sure you choose a product that is in demand and that also has very few competitors. Make sure you read the rules of the affiliate program for which you are signing up. Some affiliate programs require you to have your own Web site while others do not. When you are not required to have a Web site, you can create a blog and promote your chosen products on it.

Wholesale Seller

You have two options when it comes to starting a Web-based business in which you sell products that you have not created. You can either purchase the products you will offer to customers at a wholesale price, store the products in your home, and ship them when you receive orders or you can make use of a drop shipper, which means you only take orders and payments.

Drop shipping is a popular way for some online entrepreneurs to do business. The technicalities of drop shipping are simple: You find a product that you like and you decide to promote it. You choose how much to charge customers for the product, and you offer it to customers through your Web site. A customer purchases the product and sends you payment. Once you receive payment you purchase the product, at wholesale price, from a drop shipper. The drop shipper then packages and mails the product to your customer with your business name and business address on it. The drop shipper is a silent entity in the process, so your customers will think they are dealing directly with you.

If you decide that selling through a drop shipper is the avenue you want to pursue, your first task will be to find a product or several products you want to sell. The key to finding the ideal product or products is to research. What are popular products in your niche? What products are in demand? Are there a lot of competitors selling the product? (Keep in mind that you do not want to sell a product in a market saturated with competitors selling that same product.) For how much does the competition sell the product? Can you realistically mark the price up enough so you make a profit? Make sure you answer these questions as you conduct your research.

When you are looking for products to sell, remember to stick with products in your niche. Furthermore, limit the amount of products you sell. You do not want to overwhelm yourself, especially in the beginning.

Once you have determined what products you want to sell, you need to find a drop shipper. Be forewarned that there are plenty of scammers out there trying to make a buck from people who are looking for reputable drop shippers. You do not need to pay hundreds of dollars to another company to provide you with a list of reputable drop shippers. Just do your research. An effective way to research a drop shipper is to conduct an online search for reputable companies. Some drop shippers found online are:

- Thomas Register – **www.thomasregister.com**

- Worldwide Brands – **www.worldwidebrands.net**

- Wholesale Dropshippers Directory – **www.wholesalecentral. com/Dropshippers.html**

- World Wide Brands – **www.worldwidebrands.com**

If you are worried that a particular drop shipper sounds too good to be true, it probably is. Research the drop shipper before deciding to work with them. You might also want to check the company out at the Better Business Bureau.

After you have found a reputable drop shipper with whom you feel comfortable, you will register for an account with the drop shipper. Every drop shipping company's registration process works differently. Some will allow you to apply online or over the phone, while others require you to fill out an application and return it to the company by snail mail.

You will then start advertising the products you are going to sell on your Web site. Because you do not order the product from the drop shipper until the customer pays for it, you will want to consider using an online payment system like PayPal or Google Checkout. You can also sign up for a merchant account, which will allow you to take credit card payments. That way, you will receive payment as soon as the customer orders the product, rather than having to wait for a check or other payment form, thus increasing the time it will take for the product to be sent to the customer from the drop shipper.

Be aware that the process will not go smoothly 100 percent of the time. There will likely be times when a customer purchases a product, and when you go to order that product from your drop shipper, you will find it is sold out or the latest shipment has not yet arrived. Institute a policy for what you will do in such cases. You might offer a discount or the customer may request a refund. It is also imperative that you prepare yourself to receive refund requests. Talk with your drop shipper when you sign on with them to find out how they generally deal with returns and refunds and how it will affect your business.

Your second option is to buy at wholesale and store the products in your home until they are purchased. You must decide whether you want the extra responsibility of, and if you have the extra room for, storing and shipping your merchandise.

There are several things you must know when dealing with wholesalers. First, buying wholesale does not necessarily mean you are purchasing at the lowest price available. You may very well walk through your local shops and find the same product at lower prices simply because there is so much competition for that product.

Second, you must be aware of your competition. As mentioned earlier, entering a saturated market is going to make it much more difficult for you to make a profit than if you sell a product that is in demand but has less competition.

Just as you would if you decided to use a drop shipper, you will need to determine what products you want to sell before you do anything else. You can follow the same process you would if you were using a drop shipper:

- Research to find products in your niche.

- Once you find products you like, determine whether the market is already saturated with competition selling that product or if there is demand for the product but not enough supply.

- Limit the number of products you offer so as not to overwhelm yourself.

- Find a reputable wholesale supplier.

Research is critical in finding a reputable wholesale provider. Take the time to learn about the wholesale supplier by spending time on their Web site, paying particular attention to company policies and FAQ pages.

You may also meet representatives for wholesale suppliers at trade shows. If you do attend trade shows, make sure you take proof that you run your own Web-based business. Proof might include a business license, a resale license, your EIN number, or business cards. It is best to call ahead to find out exactly what you will need to gain admission, since most trade shows are for retailers only and do not allow the public access. Only once you have done thorough research do you want to ask any questions.

Once you find a reputable wholesale supplier you want to work with, you are going to have to set up an account with that supplier. Setting up an account with a wholesale supplier is more than just giving the company's representative your information. In fact, not all of those who request an account necessarily get one. Additionally, some wholesale suppliers simply do not work with home-based businesses. Be prepared for such an eventuality by having a list of several wholesale suppliers with whom you would like to work.

That being said, do not send out mass e-mails to suppliers with whom you are considering working. Doing so screams that you are an amateur, something you want to avoid at all costs. Rather, e-mail each wholesale supplier individually. You might want to create a basic letter you use for each wholesale supplier, but then individualize it for the specific wholesale supplier to whom you are writing.

The key to success in forging a business relationship with a wholesale supplier is to represent your Web-based business as a polished professional. Treat the wholesale supplier as you would treat potential customers: Make sure all correspondence is proofread (nothing says amateur like an error-riddled document), and have all of the pertinent information (business name, mailing address, EIN number, and all contact information) available when you talk with the wholesale supplier. Most importantly, as mentioned previously, do your research before you correspond with the wholesale supplier.

Remember, first impressions can make or break you, and that is especially true in business. You want to put your proverbial best foot forward when you deal with wholesale suppliers. You should approach your first contact as you would a job interview. You want wholesale suppliers to know you are professional and will represent their products well.

Whether you use a drop shipper or you ship products directly from your home, be sure to offer impeccable customer support. Provide customers with an easy way to get in contact with you if they have questions or if a problem arises. You can offer customer support via e-mail, live chat, or with an 800 number. (The good news is 800 numbers are extremely affordable.)

Follow up with your customers to ensure they are happy with the products they ordered and to get any feedback you can as to their experience with your company. You want them to return to you again and again, so make it a priority to answer all support communication quickly and to follow up with your customers. In short, if your customers have a problem, you have a problem, so rectify the problem as soon as possible.

Regardless of what type of Web-based business you decide to start, you will be able to implement the many marketing and advertising ideas we will discuss in later chapters.

A WORD OF CAUTION: SCAMS

When you are searching for a wholesaler or a drop shipper, you are going to run across a good chunk of companies that offer you lists of wholesalers and drop shippers for fees as high as hundreds of dollars. Never pay for a listing of drop shippers or wholesalers when you can find the information you need for free by researching online.

There are also companies online that promise to provide you with products to sell while the company will market the products. In return, you must pay steep monthly or annual fees, likely making your investment far greater than your returns. Steer clear of companies making such promises, and remember that all the information you need can be found through diligence and research.

The Internet is also ripe with scams targeting would-be entrepreneurs who want to work at home but who do not know how to get started. Even though you are starting your own Web-based business, you should be aware of these scams, should you come across them.

You have likely seen the ads littered online: promises of big money for jobs like stuffing envelopes, processing medical claims, and inputting data entry. A good rule of thumb is if it seems too good to be true, it probably is too good to be true. Alternately, if it seems too easy to be true (for example, make $5,000 a week working only eight hours a month), it probably is not on the up and up.

Being aware of scams is the first step in protecting yourself against them. The Better Business Bureau lists the most common online business/work at home scams as: assembling products at home, chain letters requesting money, stuffing envelopes, multi-level marketing, online business with ads claiming that you can make thousands online, and processing medical claims.

On a side note, it is possible to start your own medical claims processing business. However, to do so requires education, certification, experience, and the proper software.

If you suspect a scam, you can file a complaint with the Federal Trade Commission. You can contact the FTC by visiting their Web site at **www.ftc.gov**, or by calling 1-877-382-4357.

2

FINDING YOUR NICHE

Now that you know starting a Web-based business is the path you want to take, you are going to have to decide what type of business you want to start. Before you go any further, you want to identify your niche. In a very real sense, your niche will play a huge role as to whether your Web-based business flourishes or flounders.

WHAT IS A NICHE?

A niche is a narrowly defined target market. To run a successful Web-based business, you need to identify your niche and become an expert in that area. You will become an expert in your niche after you have identified your target market and have determined how you can meet your target market's needs by offering a unique product or service. Additionally, by having a strong grasp of your niche, you will be able to tailor your Web site to that specific niche.

One of the keys to your Web-based business's success is to know and understand your target market. If you do not have a clear idea of who your target market is, what your target market needs, and how to fulfill your target market's needs, your Web-based business will not be able to realize its potential.

For example, you might be a world class traveler, and you want to take that passion a bit further by starting your own Web-based business. Travel is a very broad subject, so you need to narrow it down to find your niche. What type of travel market do you want to target: Budget travelers? Luxury travelers? Senior citizen travel? Traveling with your pet? The list could go on and on.

Once you have narrowed your niche down to the type of travel you want to concentrate on, you will likely want to narrow it down even further. Say you have decided you want your niche to be budget travelers. Who are the budget travelers to whom you are marketing? Students? Women? Men? Americans? Canadians? You will want to define the demographics of your budget traveler market before you determine what type of product or service you are going to offer.

When you are researching your target market, you will want to answer the following questions:

- What is the age range of those who want or need your product or service?

- Does your product or service appeal to a specific gender or to all genders?

- What ethnicity is your target market?

- What are the typical spending and buying habits of your target market?

- What is your target market's education level? High school, some college, college graduate, graduate degree, post-graduate degree?

- What is the typical income level of your target market?

Let us get back to the example of budget travelers. In addition to understanding the demographics of your target market, you need to understand the mindset of budget travelers. Budget travelers want to find the best and most inexpensive deals on every aspect of travel: accommodation, transportation to the destination and at the destination, admission to museums and other attractions, restaurants, and so on. They also want to find great deals on products for their travel, such as backpacks, travel guides, maps, cameras, and so on.

Now that you have narrowed your niche down to budget travelers and the demographic of budget traveler, narrow it even further. What type of service or product are you going to offer to budget travelers?

Why do you want to narrow your niche? It is simple. The narrower your niche, the more sales you are going to tally. SCORE, "The Counselors to America's Small Business," suggests the best way to approach choosing a niche is to find out what niches are currently underserved or not served at all and cater to that niche. Or you might want to create a whole new niche.

Keep this word of caution in mind, however: While you want to narrow your niche down, you want to ensure you do not want to make it so narrow that you have a very small market.

WHAT INTERESTS YOU?

Find a niche that excites you. Remember, you are going to be putting considerable time into building your Web-based business, and you do not want to be stuck with a niche that you do not enjoy or that bores you. Finding a niche that excites you will make going to work in your home office every day that much more enjoyable and will motivate you that much more.

But your niche must do much more than excite you. It must fill a need in the market, be unique, and stand out from your competition. Make sure you identify what makes your Web-based business unique and how your product or service is going to outshine the competition.

A word of warning, however: The "how to make money on the Internet" niche is saturated, and you should steer clear of it. In fact, there are several well-known Internet marketers who actually do make money on the Internet, whose products are incredibly popular. The only instance in which you should consider entering the niche is if you actually have made money on the Internet and can prove you have done so.

However, you can get a slice of the action with those popular Internet marketers by signing up as an affiliate and promoting their products, which we discussed in Chapter One.

Before you begin to research potential niches in which you might want to work, take an assessment of yourself. You can do this quickly and easily by making three lists:

1. Your skills — In which skills and/or talents are you strongest? How can you make use of those skills in a Web-based business?

2. Your areas of expertise

3. Subjects about which you are passionate

Your list should give you insight into your areas of interest and highlight possible niches in which you would like to specialize.

RESEARCH

Now that you have a list of your skills, your areas of expertise, and subjects about which you are passionate, you will be able to narrow your list down to potential niches. Once you have done that, you are going to ask yourself several questions to determine if the niche is right for you. First, however, write down your niche and the specific product or service you plan to provide. Then answer these simple questions:

1. Is there a need for your product or service that is currently not being met?

2. Is there a large demand for your product or service but not enough of a supply to meet the demand?

3. Is your product or service going to be competitive within your target market?

4. Who is your target market?

5. What does your product or service bring to the market that the competition does not?

Answer these questions, but go a step further by listing each of the reasons potential customers will want to purchase your product or service rather than the one being offered by your competition. Once you have written that list, you are going to start another list, this time listing each reason prospective customers may have for not purchasing your product or service.

Again, you must understand your target market, so you can tailor your Web site and your product to your prospective customers. Once you have pinpointed your niche and your target market, you will be ready to start planning your Web-based business by writing your business plan.

3

WRITING YOUR BUSINESS PLAN

Your business plan is the roadmap that will help guide you and your Web-based business toward profit and success. It will also help you stay on track and keep your sights clearly focused on your business goals. Your business plan is the key ingredient to your business success. It outlines a definition of your business, your business goals, your marketing strategies, your public relations and advertising goals, and how you are going to manage your Web-based business.

Should you determine that you need to secure financial funds to start or to grow your business, you will need a strong, clear business plan to show banks and other lenders. Before you go any further with your Web-based business, make writing your business plan a top priority.

The good news is a business plan is not difficult to write. Every business plan follows a simple formula as outlined below:

BUSINESS PLAN OUTLINE
I. Cover sheet
II. Statement of purpose
III. Table of contents
A. Your Business
• A description of your business
• Marketing
• The competition

BUSINESS PLAN OUTLINE

- Employees
- Insurance for the business
- Financial data

B. Financial Data
- Applications for loans
- Equipment you will need
- Balance sheet
- Profit analysis
- Profit and loss statements:
  - Summary for the first three years
  - Month-by-month detail for the first year
  - Quarter-by-quarter detail for the following two years
  - "Assumptions upon which projects were based"
  - Pro-forma cash flow

C. Supporting Documents
- Principals' tax returns for the previous three years
- Your personal financial statement (you can find the required forms at any bank
- One copy of your business license, other required licenses, and other relevant legal documents
- One copy of each principal's resume
- Copies of letters of intent from your product's suppliers (if applicable)

STEP-BY-STEP: THE FINER POINTS OF THE BUSINESS PLAN

Before you can begin work on your business plan, you need to know what must go in the business plan. Unfortunately, it is not uncommon for many new and prospective Web-based business owners to overlook this very important aspect of starting a business.

You will want to start by dividing your business plan into five sections: 1. the executive summary, 2. a description of your business, 3. the marketing plan, 4. the management plan, and 5. the financial management plan. Your business plan will also include financial projects and any relevant supporting documents.

The Executive Summary

The executive summary of your business plan is the first thing prospective lenders, and anyone else who reads your business plan, will see. However, it is going to be the last part of the business plan that you actually write, and you should keep it as succinct as possible. Do your best to ensure the executive summary does not exceed four pages.

In short, the executive summary is the single most important component of your business plan. It succinctly summarizes your business plan, and it informs readers about your plans for your Web-based business.

The executive summary should include:

- A mission statement summarizing the purpose of your Web-based business.

- The date your business began.

- The names of all of the owners and their titles.

- A list of the products or services you offer.

- A brief explanation of how your product or service will fill a need with your target market.

- A brief description of your experience and how your product or service is unique in the market.

The executive summary also contains vital information including the business name, the business address, business telephone number, business fax number, and business e-mail.

Take the time that is needed to develop a strong executive summary. Even if you do not think anyone but you is going to look at your business plan, write it as though others will be reading and judging your Web-based business based on your business plan. A situation may arise where you need a business plan, so it is best to have one written and ready for such occasions. Keep that old cliché, "If you fail to plan, you plan to fail," in mind as you move forward with your Web-based business.

Your Business Description

Your business description is likely the first part of the business plan on which you are going to work. It should succinctly but thoroughly describe your Web-based business. The business description also provides you with the opportunity to think about your Web-based business's primary focus.

The thought of creating a succinct description may cause you some anxiety, but it is actually an important exercise that is not as difficult as you might imagine. Start by considering what products or services your Web-based business will offer, your target market, and why your business stands apart from the competition. Keep in mind that your business plan is not set in stone, and you can and should modify it as needed.

You will divide your business description into three parts. In the first section, you will describe your business in detail. In the second section, describe your product or service. Finally, in the third section, focus on your business location. For a Web-based business, you will likely be operating out of your home office, rather than actually renting or purchasing office space or storage space, if you are offering a physical product.

Your business description should include an explanation of each of the following:

1. **Legalities**. Mention any business licenses or permits you will need to legally operate your Web-based business.

2. **Business-type**. Describe which legal business type you have chosen: sole proprietorship, partnership, LLC (Limited Liability Company), S Corporation, or corporation.

3. **Your product or service**. Discuss your product or service.

4. **Your business character**. Is your Web-based business a startup or are you purchasing an already-established business? Will your business be affiliate-related? Will you sell products to your customers? If that is the path you want to take, will you use a drop shipper or will you purchase products at wholesale and sell them directly to your customers?

5. **Reasons your Web-based business will be profitable**. Why is your Web-based business going to make money? What growth opportunities are available for your Web-based business?

6. **Your business's opening day**. Explain when your Web-based business will open its virtual doors for customers.

7. **Lessons learned**. Discuss what you have learned from your research about starting and running a Web-based business from outside sources, such as other Web-based business owners, online and offline publications, and trade suppliers. You should also consider contacting SCORE (found on the Web at **www.score.org**) or the Small Business Administration (found online at **www.sba.gov**). Both offer valuable counseling and advice for small business owners, often for free. SCORE is comprised of retired business owners who lead seminars (for a fee) on how to start a small business and meet with entrepreneurs for counseling on their small business ideas.

Use your Web-based business description to explain how your Web-based business is unique from similar Web-based businesses and how your product or service is going to appeal to online consumers.

Ensure that your business description is clearly focused on your goals, and explain why you have decided to or have already started a Web-based business.

Product or Service

Put yourself in your potential customers' shoes and then describe each of the benefits your customers will enjoy when using your product or service. If you want to be successful, you must know or have an idea about what your customers are going to expect from your Web-based business. When you know what your customers expect, you will have a much easier time ensuring customer satisfaction, which, in turn, will help you build customer loyalty. Additionally, knowing what your customers expect will help you either remain competitive or, in the best scenario, will ensure you stay ahead of the competition.

In this section, you want to describe:

- The product(s) or service(s) your Web-based business will be selling.

- The benefits of your product or service to your customers.

- The specific products or services out of all the products or services you offer that are going to be in demand.

- How your Web-based business's product or service is unique.

Location

Unlike traditional brick-and-mortar businesses that can literally live or die based on their location, Web-based businesses do not generally have to worry about a physical location, at least at first, even if you are going to be reselling a product, in conjunction with a drop shipper, directly to your customers. Still, virtual location is important. Your domain name and URL are going to be your address online, so you have to make them memorable.

Finally, you do not need to be a professional writer to write a clear, thorough, professional business plan. To ensure you do not overlook anything in your business plan, consider creating a checklist of what you need to cover. After you have finished a topic, cross it off. It may add a few more minutes to the time it takes you to write your business plan, but it will ultimately be well worth the time and the effort.

The Marketing Plan

Marketing is absolutely essential to the success of any business — online or offline. If you want to succeed, you must market your Web-based business. The key ingredient of successful marketing is knowing your customers — what they expect from your Web-based business, what they like, what they dislike, and who they are (i.e. age group, education level, income level, interests, etc.). If you take the time to identify each of these aspects, you will be able to develop an effective marketing plan that will allow you to identify and meet your customers' needs.

Who are your customers? Consider this question when determining your base customers' age, sex, income, educational level, and where your average customer resides. When you first begin marketing your Web-based business, focus your attention on targeting those customers who are most likely to buy your product or service. Once your business begins to grow, your customer base will likely expand beyond your original target market. When that happens, consider tweaking your marketing plan to include your new customers.

You can start developing your marketing plan — which will be a part of your overall business plan — by taking the time to answer several important questions, including:

- What is your target market(s)? Essentially, you want to determine who your customers are likely to be.

- Is your market(s) growing? Shrinking? Or is it an overall steady market?

- How are you going to promote sales?

- How do you plan to gain, hold, or increase the market share of your product or service?

- What pricing strategy are you going to use to determine your product's or service's prices?

The Competition

Every business has competition. Expect it and prepare for it. The good news is your Web-based business can not only stand apart from the competition, but it can beat the competition, if you know what you are doing and you offer a superior product or service.

Unfortunately, business success is never a guarantee, even with all the advances in technology that Web-based business owners have at their fingertips. It is not unheard of or uncommon for a Web-based business to be on fire one day and flailing the next.

Understand that your Web-based business will be entering a highly competitive arena, but the key to success is knowing and understanding your competition. When working on "The Competition" section of your business plan, you must:

- Determine the five Web-based businesses that are your closest direct competition.

- Identify the five Web-based businesses that are your closest indirect competition.

- Evaluate and determine if each Web-based business's business is: holding steady, increasing, or declining.

- Make a list of what you have learned from each business's operations and advertising.

- Identify the strengths and the weaknesses of each of the ten businesses.

- Determine how each of the business's products or services is different from your product or service.

Take the time to research your competition now, and keep up with what they are doing even after your Web-based business is successful. Since all your competitors are going to be Web-based, start a separate folder (using a word processing program) on your hard drive for each of your top ten competitors. Use this folder to gather information on your competition: how they advertise and promote their products or services, when they offer sales, and what techniques they use for pricing their products or services.

To reiterate, you do not want to start and compile these folders and then simply forget about them. You want to review and add to them periodically. Check out your competitors' Web content and sales content: Does it grab your attention? Is it concise and clear? Or is it long and rambling? When your competitors offer their products or services at a reduced price, how do they announce the sale? Is it splashed on the first page the Web site visitor clicks onto? Or is it shown by the original price of the product?

Take the time to study your competitors. Understanding who they are and how they operate will only help you create more effective marketing, advertising, and public relations.

A word of warning: Remember to always back up your hard drive periodically. There is nothing more frustrating and senseless than spending weeks, or even months, working on a project or researching the competition then losing it all in mere seconds. A backup will protect your hard work.

Pricing and Sales

Consumers want a quality product or service at competitive prices. Another effective marketing technique is your sales strategy. An effective sales strategy can help you retain competitiveness online. Before you create your sales strategy, study your top ten competitors. What type of strategy are they using? Researching your competitions' sales strategies will help you determine if your prices are competitive for your target market.

When you develop your sales strategy, you must take several factors into consideration, including:

- Cost of product or service

- Costs for overhead

- Costs for materials

- Pricing below your competition

- Pricing above your competition

Your Web-based business's success is dependent upon a strong sales and pricing strategy. You must also ensure you constantly check prices and compare them to your operating costs to ensure you are making a profit. You must make it a priority to stay on top of the marketplace to ensure your prices remain competitive.

Advertising and Public Relations

There are literally millions of Web-based businesses, all competing for customers. You can have the most efficient, competitively-priced product or service on the Internet, but if you are not actively advertising your product or service, you are never going to win new customers and ultimately have a successful Web-based business.

Do not allow yourself to fall prey to the notion that your product or service is so superior that it will simply sell itself. Web-based business owners who work under that philosophy generally are not business owners for very long. The good news is you can advertise and promote your Web-based business's product or service for less money than you may imagine, especially when you are in the startup phase. We will discuss, in-depth, the many ways you can promote your product or service in upcoming chapters.

Have an advertising and public relations plan. Even though your business is based online, you can network and promote your business offline as well, so consider that when you create your advertising and public relations campaign. Remember to keep your Web site and other advertising and promotional material concise, catchy, and descriptive. In essence, your marketing plan is the backbone of your Web-based business, so devote enough time and attention to it.

The Management Plan

The attraction of a self-owned Web-based business for many is the ability it offers you to be your own boss. While that may be a great incentive, it is also important to remember that managing your own business requires hard work, strong decision-making skills, persistence, and dedication. You must also know how to manage your Web-based business's finances and employees. The management plan is the foundation upon which your Web-based business's success is built.

For offline businesses, employees are a necessity. However, for your Web-based business, you do not need to hire employees, especially in the startup stages. Employees, though, may become a consideration as your business thrives and grows. For the sake of this section, however, we are going to go with the assumption that you will be hiring employees.

Employees are the backbone of every business. If you hire employees for your Web-based business, they will complement your areas of weakness. For example, if you are weak in Web content, you may consider hiring a professional writer or a freelance writer to create compelling content for you.

To know exactly what holes you need employees to fill, you must identify the skills you need but do not have. If you cannot acquire those skills on your own, consider hiring or contracting someone who does have those skills.

When you hire employees, you will need to know how to manage them, but you will also need to treat them as respected members of your team. When you make changes that affect the business, ask your employees for their opinions. Your employees can be an invaluable source of new ideas and different ways of thinking, which can positively impact your Web-based business.

When you write your management plan, ask yourself the following questions:

- In what ways are your business experience and your overall background an asset to your Web-based business?

- What weaknesses do you have?

- How can you compensate for those weaknesses?

- Of whom will the management team be comprised (if applicable)?

- What are your management team's strengths and weaknesses?

- What are your management team's responsibilities within your Web-based business?

- Are the management team's individual responsibilities clearly defined in a written document?

- Will those on your management team be ongoing members of your business or will they only be on board during the startup phase?

- What, if any, are your current personnel needs?

- How will you hire personnel?

- How will you train personnel?

- What type of salary, vacation, and holiday pay will you offer your employees?

- Can you offer any benefits — health insurance, for example — to your employees at this point in your Web-based business's life?

Keep in mind that employees will likely not even be a consideration during the startup of your Web-based business and, in fact, you may be able to run your business solo as long as you have it. Still, knowing what to expect if and when you need employees is a good idea.

The Financial Management Plan

If you want your Web-based business to become and remain profitable, you must have a solid financial management plan. You must be able to effectively manage your finances if you want your Web-based business to succeed. Every year thousands of businesses, with potential for success, fold. Why? Because their owners either did not know how to effectively manage their business's finances or simply failed to do so. You can avoid such failure by creating a financial management plan that will ensure you meet your financial obligations.

In most instances, Web-based business startups have lower overhead than traditional brick and mortar businesses. Still, you must determine what costs you will have at startup and what costs you will incur when operating your Web-based business. Once you know those costs, you will be able to better create a budget for your business.

Creating your startup budget is the first component of your financial management plan. Some of the costs in your startup budget will be one-time costs. For example, your computer or Web design software will likely be a one-time cost. Take these types of costs into consideration when working on your startup budget.

Other startup expenses may include:

- Computer equipment
- Licenses/permits
- Web host
- Insurance
- High-speed Internet setup
- Supplies
- Business accounting software
- Advertising
- Web design software
- Legal or professional fees

The second component of your financial management plan is your operating budget, which will be important when you open your business. However, you do not need to actually develop your operating budget until you are ready to launch your Web-based business.

The SBA recommends that every small business's operating budget includes enough money to cover all projected expenses for the first three to six months of business.

Operating expenses may include:

- Web hosting
- Taxes
- High-speed Internet
- Insurance
- Equipment
- Advertising

In addition to your startup and operating budgets, the financial management plan should also include loan applications, a list of supplies, a startup equipment list, a balance sheet, a profit and loss statement (income projections), and a pro-forma cash flow and break-even analysis. A three year summary will be included in your cash flow projection and income projection. The first year will be detailed month-by-month with the following two years being detailed quarter-by-quarter.

The financial management plan also consists of how you will undertake the accounting for your Web-based business.

In addition, answer the following questions:

- What accounting system or software will you use to keep track of your sales either directly or through a drop shipper?

- What financial projects will be included in your business plan?

- What are your goals for sales and profits for the year?

- If you are selling a product, which you purchased from a wholesaler, what type of inventory-control system will you put into place?

- What payment methods will you accept from customers?

LEGAL BUSINESS ENTITIES

You cannot legally operate your Web-based business until you file your legal business entity with the state in which you reside and in which your business will be run. One of the key decisions you are going to make when starting your Web-based business is what type of business structure you want to operate under.

The Small Business Administration, an invaluable resource for prospective and current small business owners, recommends consulting an accountant or an attorney to help you decide which type of ownership best suits your needs because your decision will affect your business in the long-term.

When deciding which business structure to use, you will need to consider several factors, including:

- How big do you hope to grow your Web-based business?

- How much control over the business do you want to have?

- What are the tax implications of each ownership structure?

- Will you need to invest your earnings back into your business?

- What level of vulnerability are you willing to leave your business open to?

- What are your business's expected profits and losses?

Following you will learn about the different types of business structures, including the advantages and disadvantages of each.

Sole Proprietorship

Forming a sole proprietorship is actually one of the most popular business structures. In fact, many small businesses actually begin as sole proprietorships. Sole proprietorships have a single owner, and that person generally runs and manages the business. As a result, the owner receives all of the business's profit and owns all of the business's assets.

There are numerous other advantages to forming a sole proprietorship, including:

- In addition to being the easiest structure to form, it is also the cheapest business structure.

- The sole proprietor makes all the decisions for his or her business.

- The sole proprietor pays taxes on profits on his or her individual tax return.

- Dissolving a sole proprietorship is generally easy.

One of the downsides to the sole proprietorship is the owner is legally responsible for the business's debts and liabilities. Sole proprietors are the business. If you are a sole proprietor, you are legally responsible for all debts, have unlimited liability, and your personal and business assets can be seized to pay debts.

Additional disadvantages to sole proprietorships include:

- You may not be able to secure business loans. Instead, you will have to apply for consumer loans or dip into your personal savings.

- If you decide to purchase health insurance, your premiums will be considered an adjustment to your overall income.

Partnerships

Partnerships are just what the name implies. A single business is owned by two or more people. Partnerships are similar to sole proprietorships in that the owners are not legally separate from their businesses. For a partnership to be successful, the owners should have an operating agreement, or another legal document, that clearly defines distribution of profits, protocol for resolving disputes and bringing new partners into the business, and the procedure for buying partners out.

Advantages to forming a partnership include:

- The most time consuming aspect of forming a partnership will be creating your partnership agreement. Otherwise, partnerships are rather simple to form.

- Raising money for the business should conceivably be easier because the partnership has at least two owners.

- The partners pay taxes on the profits on their individual tax returns.

Among the disadvantages of a partnership are:

- Each partner is legally responsible for the other partners' actions.

- You have to share your profits with the other partners.

- There is the distinct possibility of internal conflict because decisions must be agreed upon by all partners.

- Partnerships can legally be dissolved should a partner pull out of the business or die.

Corporations

Unlike sole proprietorships and partnerships, a corporation is a separate entity from its owners. That means the corporation pays the business taxes, is liable for any lawsuits, and has the ability to enter into contracts. In the eyes of the law, corporation owners are referred to as share owners. The corporation is run by a board of directors, who are elected by the shareholders, and make all of the decisions and set policies. Corporations do not dissolve upon an owner's death or withdrawal from the business.

Some of the advantages of a corporation are:

- The debts of and the judgments against the corporation affects the shareholders minimally as they only hold limited liability.

- A corporation's shareholders are generally responsible only for stock investments in the company.

- To raise funds, corporations are able to sell stocks.

- Corporations that meet specific requirements can claim S status. S status corporations are taxed in the same way as partnerships.

Disadvantages of a corporation include:

- Incorporating a business is a more costly and time consuming process than forming a sole proprietorship or partnership.

- Federal and state agencies closely monitor corporations, which means the business may have to complete much more paperwork to stay in compliance with regulations.

- In some instances, corporations are required to pay higher taxes than other business structures.

Limited Liability Company

The newest business structure, the Limited Liability Company (LLC), is now legally permitted in all of the United States and is one of the most popular business structures for small business owners. The LLC allows for owners to have limited liability, like the owners of a corporation have, while enjoying the same tax structure and flexibility in operating the business that partnerships afford.

Advantages of a Limited Liability Company include:

- Owners of an LLC enjoy personal liability protection.

- An LLC is not as formal as a corporation, which allows LLC owners flexibility in managing the business.

- Owners of an LLC decide how they want to divide profits unlike a partnership, which requires each partner to receive 50 percent of the profits.

- LLCs can have an unlimited number of members.

Among the disadvantages of a Limited Liability Company are:

- If an LLC member declares bankruptcy or dies, the LLC is effectively dissolved.

- Each member of the LLC generally has to pay self-employment taxes.

- When creating an LLC, you will have to fill out more complex paperwork than you would for a sole proprietorship or a partnership.

Now you should have at least some idea of the type of business structure that will be best for your Web-based business. However, you should consult with an accountant or a lawyer to determine if the business structure you are considering is the best for your needs. Remember, choosing the right business structure is essential because the choice has long-term implications as to how your business can and must be run.

4

LEGAL CONSIDERATIONS

Starting a business takes a lot of work, and there are numerous legal requirements you will have to fulfill before you can legally begin operating your business, including choosing a name for your business, registering your business name, deciding what type of business entity your Web-based business should register as, and applying for all necessary permits.

The process of legally starting your Web-based business generally is not a long or arduous process, but it is essential that you complete all of the legal requirements before opening your virtual business doors.

CHOOSING A NAME FOR YOUR WEB-BASED BUSINESS

Choosing a name for your business is crucial, and it could literally mean the difference between success and failure. The most important thing to remember when naming your business is not to go with the first name that pops into your mind. Rather, take the time to really think about what you want your business's name to convey.

Some Web-based entrepreneurs simply use a combination of their legal name and the professional service or product they offer. For example, professional writer John Doe may decide to name his professional writing service John Doe Professional Writing. Or Jane Doe, who creates gift baskets, might call her business Jane Doe's Unique Gift Baskets.

Other Web-based entrepreneurs prefer coming up with a unique name. To start the process, invite your friends and family to a brainstorming session. Add as many potential names to the list as you can, keeping in mind to ensure the business name is:

- Meaningful. The name should encapsulate the core aspects of your business.

- Easy to pronounce.

- Easy to understand.

- Attention grabbing.

- Spelled like it sounds.

- Easy to remember.

You also want to make sure you choose a name that can grow as your business grows. That means you do not want your business name to be too narrow. For example, let us say you have decided to start a Web-based business selling cookie baskets, so you decide to name your business Creative Cookies. Perhaps as your business grows, however, you want to expand your product offerings to candy, cakes, and other baked goods. You would have to consider whether the name Creative Cookies gives your business enough room to grow.

Once you have chosen a name that you think suits your Web-based business, you will have to register it with your local and state government.

REGISTERING YOUR BUSINESS NAME

One of the first things you will want to do to get your Web-based business kicked off is to name it. But there is more to naming your business than just deciding what you are going to call it. Before you legally name your business, you will need to know what business structure you are using: sole proprietor, partnership, LLC, or corporation.

If your business entity is either a sole proprietorship or a partnership, you will be operating under your own name, at least in the eyes of the law. So, if your name is Jane Doe and you have a quilt-making business, your business name may be Jane Doe Quilts. However, not all sole proprietors and partnerships want to work under the business owner(s)'s name. Many sole proprietors and partnerships decide instead to operate under an assumed or a fictitious name, like their LLC and corporation counterparts.

Following are the general rules for registering your business name.

Sole Proprietorship

If you choose to use a fictitious name for your sole proprietorship, you will need to file a fictitious owner affidavit at your county recorder of deeds office. The affidavit is simply a legal form that reveals the owner of the sole proprietorship and the name the business is working under. The affidavit is open to both the public and the local government.

Partnership

As with a sole proprietorship, it is just assumed that your business will be run under your name. If you choose to run your business under a fictitious name, you will need to file an affidavit with your county recorder of deeds office. In some instances, partnerships are required to file their assumed name affidavit with their state's Secretary of State. Check with your local county recorder of deeds office or your Secretary of State to determine where you must file your affidavit.

Limited Liability Company

If your business structure is that of a Limited Liability Company, you will have to go through a more formal process of registering your business's name. If your business is a Limited Liability Company, you will have to include the LLC in your business name in some form — for example: My Business LLC, My Business LC, My Business Limited Liability Company. Check with your Secretary of State's office to determine the exact requirements.

Generally, you will reserve your LLC name with your state when you file your business's articles of organization. The name and articles of organization are filed with the Secretary of State's office.

Your articles of organization will be rejected by your Secretary of State if the name you have chosen is already being used by another LLC. You can either phone your state's Secretary of State office or visit their Web site to determine if the name you want is already in use.

Corporation

When you choose your corporation name, you will have to file it with your Secretary of State, and you must ensure that there is not another corporation using the same business name. If there is, the Secretary of State will reject your articles of incorporation. Your corporation name must include either corporation, incorporated, company, or limited. Or you can use "Inc." or "Corp."

Note that if your corporation is an S corporation, you do not have to identify it as such in your business name. The only time it is required to identify your business as an S corporation is when you file your state and federal taxes.

You can determine if the name you want to use is either already reserved or being used by calling your Secretary of State's office or by visiting their Web site to search business names. If the name you want to use is available, you may be able to reserve it through your Secretary of State's office.

You can find your Secretary of State's office on their Web site, State and Local Government on the Net, found at **www.statelocalgov.net/50states-secretary-state.cfm**.

Regardless of what business entity you have established, you may want to consider registering your name with the United States Trademark and Patent Office, especially if you are planning to grow on a larger scale, rather than the business remaining solely in your state.

Start by visiting the U.S. Trademark and Patent Office and doing a nationwide search to determine if the name you want to use is available. You can find the U.S. Trademark and Patent Office online at **www.uspto.gov/main/trademarks.htm**.

BUSINESS LICENSES REQUIRED BY YOUR CITY/STATE

Business license requirements vary from state to state. However, businesses generally have to file for a business license that will allow them to operate legally in their particular city and/or state. Business licenses come with a minimal fee, and you can find out about your city's and state's particular requirements by visiting your local city hall's Web site and your Secretary of State's Web site.

Home Occupation Permit

If you will be running your Web-based business from home, you will likely need a home occupation permit. Most cities require home-based businesses to pay either a percentage of their annual profits or to pay an annual flat fee.

Contact your local city hall to determine if you need a home occupation permit and how to apply for one if you do.

Zoning Permit

Some locales require a zoning permit for home-based businesses. Contact your local city hall to find out if there are zoning requirements for those in your area running home-based businesses.

Additionally, if you rent a condominium or live in a home in a homeowner's association, you will have to speak to the relevant person to determine if home-based businesses are allowed. It is not uncommon for landlords and homeowner's associations to forbid or restrict home-based businesses.

Local Business Permit

Most cities and towns require home-based business owners to apply for a local business permit, which must be renewed annually. Contact your local city hall to determine whether you must apply for a local business permit. You can also check out your local government's Web site to get more information on what permit(s) you will be required to file.

Before you can apply for a local business permit, you will need your EIN number and evidence that you have reserved or registered your fictitious business name, if you have one. Most cities and towns also require an application fee.

Resale Permit

Depending on the laws in your state, you may also need a resale license to sell products from your home. The actual name of the resale license may vary, as different states call it different names, but essentially the names are all equal. It may also be called a seller's permit, a resale certificate, a resale number, a certificate of authority, a resale permit, use and sales tax license, permit sales and use tax, transaction privilege sales tax, or application to collect/report tax.

The permit, which is generally issued by the State Franchise Board, is important because it allows you to purchase wholesale without having to pay tax on your purchases. Sales taxes are then paid by the customers who purchase the products. The one stipulation to the resale permit is you must use it to purchase products that you will resale to consumers; it may not be used to purchase wholesale products for personal use.

A resale permit may not be required if your home-based business is a corporate entity. In that case, you can use your federal tax identification to purchase wholesale products you will resale.

Contact your local city hall or your local Chamber of Commerce to find out whether a resale permit is required in your state and how to apply for that resale permit.

Sales Tax

Should you be providing a product that is subject to sales tax, you will need to charge your customers' sales tax and then pay that sales tax to the appropriate city, county, or state agencies. (Your resale permit will allow you to do this while also allowing you not to have to pay sales tax.)

As a side note, there are several states that do not charge sales tax: Alaska, Delaware, Montana, New Hampshire, and Oregon. Still, some of the cities and towns have their own sales tax while Delaware, Montana, New Hampshire, and Oregon require sales taxes on certain types of transactions.

Statement of Work/Contract

If you are offering a professional service, such as consulting or Web design, you should seriously consider having a formal statement of work or contract written to protect both you and your clients.

Essentially, a statement of work/contract outlines what you are to do for your client and should include:

- Your name, your business name, business address, and contact information.

- Your client's name, address, and contact information.

- The service you will provide for the client – be specific when you describe exactly what you are going to do for the client.

- The fee for the service you will be providing.

- How (Paypal, GoogleCheckout, e-check, etc.) and when the client will pay for services rendered.

- Estimated time of delivery of the service being provided.

- The duration of the contract.

- Any additional terms, including under what circumstances either you or the client can cancel the project.

The statement of work/contract should be signed by you and the client, dated by each of you, and each of you should have a copy before work begins.

You can hire a lawyer to prepare a statement of work/contract for use with your Web-based business. If you cannot afford a lawyer, especially in the beginning, you can find business books with sample contracts that you can use.

EMPLOYER IDENTIFICATION NUMBER (EIN)

Even if you do not intend to hire employees, you are legally obligated to obtain an Employer Identification Number unless you have registered your business as a sole proprietor. Employer Identification Numbers are used to recognize business entities and are issued by the Internal Revenue Service (IRS).

Applying for an EIN number is easy, fast, and free. You can apply for an EIN in several ways:

- **By phone** - 800-829-4933. Simply call the toll-free number anytime Monday through Friday between the hours of 7 a.m. and 3 p.m. local time. You will answer several questions, and by the end of your phone call, you will receive your EIN number.

- **By fax** – To find the fax number relevant to your state, visit the IRS page **www.irs.gov/file/article/0,,id=111453,00.html**. To apply for an EIN number by fax, you will be required to fill out IRS Form SS-4 (found at **https://sa2.www4.irs.gov/sa_vign/ newFormSS4.do**). The IRS will review the form and determine if your business needs an EIN number. If it does, you will receive your EIN number within four business days, provided you give the IRS a fax number.

- **Online** – You can apply for your EIN number by filling out Form SS-4 which you can find online at **https://sa2.www4.irs. gov/sa_vign/newFormSS4.do**. Once you have completed the form and hit the submit button, you will be informed if you have left out any pertinent information. As soon as you have submitted the completed application, you will receive an EIN number.

- **By mail** – If you want to send your EIN application in by mail, you will have to wait approximately four weeks to receive your EIN number.

A new EIN number is required when a business changes ownership or if the structure of your business changes (for example, from a partnership to a LLC). To learn more about the requirements for needing a new EIN number, visit the IRS's Web site, specifically **www.irs.gov/businesses/ small/article/0,,id=98011,00.html**.

If you misplace or lose your EIN number, call 800-829-4933 Monday through Friday 7 a.m. to 3 p.m. local time. To save you the headache of losing your EIN number, keep it in a secure place in your office and on your computer.

FTC REGULATIONS THAT WILL IMPACT HOW YOU DO BUSINESS ONLINE

Spam

As a responsible business owner, you must be aware of the laws and regulations with which you will be legally required to comply. One of the biggest problems on the Internet is the problem with companies sending out spam, which is essentially non-solicited advertising and promotional e-mails. If you have a free e-mail account, from a company like Yahoo or Hotmail, you likely receive dozens, if not hundreds, of spam e-mails every week. Spam is one of the biggest nuisances on the Internet.

Not only does it annoy potential customers, but it is also against the law. Avoid sending spam at all costs. In fact, the Federal Trade Commission (FTC) has begun cracking down hard on those businesses and companies that spam consumers. The FTC passed the CAN-SPAM Act 2003 on January 1, 2004. In a nutshell, this federal act targets those companies that send mass e-mails advertising or marketing either a service or a commercial product.

Regardless of what type of Web-based business you start, you must have a strong grasp of what you are not allowed to do according to the CAN-SPAM Act of 2003.

- You must be honest in who you are when sending e-mails. That is, your e-mail header must show the originating e-mail address and domain, including the name of the originating sender.

- Your subject line must be forthright about what the e-mail contains. Misleading subjects are illegal.

- You must provide those receiving your e-mails an option for opting out of your mailing list. You must then take those recipients, who have requested you no longer send them e-mails, off of your list within ten business days, according to the law. Failure to do so can result in hefty fines.

- You must include your business mailing address in all of your commercial e-mails.

- You cannot sell or give others' the e-mail addresses of those who opted out as your recipient. To do so is illegal.

The Federal Trade Commission does not take spammers' actions lightly, and those businesses that send spam will face fines of as much as $11,000. Spammers also face additional fines for:

- Using automation or scripts to sign up for more than one e-mail account in an attempt to send commercial e-mails.

- Creating e-mails by randomly using letters and numbers. The FTC refers to this method, used by some businesses, as "a dictionary attack."

You can find full disclosure of the CAN-SPAM Act of 2003 on the Federal Trade Commission's Web site at **www.ftc.gov/bcp/conline/pubs/buspubs/ canspam.htm** or you can visit **www.ftc.gov/spam** for FTC updates to the law. As a Web-based business owner, you must know what you are and are not allowed to do in terms of advertising and promotions. Otherwise, you could face strict consequences.

FTC's Prompt Delivery Rules

If you are selling a product to customers online, over the phone, or via fax, you will have to comply with the FTC's prompt delivery rules. First, for your advertising and promotional material to contain a timeframe of delivery of products to customers, you must have what the FTC defines as a "reasonable basis" for providing that timeframe. Likewise, if your advertising or promotional materials have not made a promise of delivery timeframe, you must have a "reasonable basis" as to how the product can be delivered within 30 days.

If you do not meet your promised shipping date or if you do not ship the product within 30 days (if your advertising and promotional materials did not state a timeframe for delivery), you must inform your customer that there will be a delay and give a new shipping time. You must also inform your customer that he has the right to cancel the order, and you will provide him with a quick refund.

If you are certain there will be a delay of as many as 30 days, you must inform the customer. Should the customer not respond, his silence is considered an agreement to the delay. Should you have an indefinite delay or a delay of longer than 30 days, you are legally required to have the customer give you his or her agreement — either in a written statement, an e-mail, or verbally. If consent is not given by the customer, you are required to refund the money, regardless of whether the customer asks for a refund or not.

You do, however, have the legal right to cancel any orders that you do not think you can deliver in a fair timeframe.

Privacy Disclosures

Many Web-based businesses, and other Web sites, collect personal data from customers and Web site visitors. Because of the concern over what personal information is used for and how personal information is protected, many of those with Web sites provide privacy statements or disclosures that detail why the information is collected, how it is used, with whom it is shared, and how it is kept secure.

When you publish a privacy policy for your customers, you must enforce it. Section 5 of the FTC Act protects consumers against unfair and/or deceptive practices, which includes privacy policies that are not enforced. The FTC is serious about Web site owners honoring their privacy policies, and those that do not face legal consequences.

On a side note, by offering your customers a privacy policy, and by enforcing it, you are laying the foundation of trust between your business and your customers. Ultimately, trust is one of consumers' top concerns.

Truth in Advertising

Truth in advertising is the law in advertising — both online and offline. Make that your personal motto when it comes to advertising. According to the Federal Trade Commission Act, deceptive and/or unfair advertising is illegal.

If you plan to advertise, you must ensure your advertisements are not deceptive. Deception occurs when an advertisement misleads potential customers and when customers' decisions and/or behavior, regarding the product or service you are offering, are affected.

If you are going to advertise, you must make sure any claims you make about your product or service are substantiated. As a Web-based business owner, you will be responsible for any claims you make about your product or service. You will also be responsible, if you promise to provide refunds for unsatisfied customers, to make those refunds.

Additionally, if you put any disclaimers or disclosures on your Web site, you must ensure they are easy-to-understand and are in a place where customers will easily notice them.

The Importance of Copyrights

Copyright is an extremely important topic, and one of which you should at least have a basic understanding, especially if you have a Web-based business. First, copyright only protects certain entities, such as original works of poetry, short stories, novels, other literary forms, songs, films, architecture, and computer software.

However, copyright does not protect everything, including ideas. For example, you may be a freelance writer and have an idea for an article that you pitch to a magazine. The magazine may reject your query then have a staff writer write the article. Unfortunately, you have no recourse because you cannot copyright an idea.

Copyright also does not protect facts, forms of operation, and systems.

Keep the copyright rules in mind when you create your Web content or hire a professional writer to provide Web content for you. Unfortunately, there is a huge problem of plagiarism online, and there are those unscrupulous Web masters who steal content from one Web site and use it as their own.

Copyright theft can carry a hefty fine, so make sure all of the content you use on your Web site is original. You can also check regularly to see if your Web site's content, or other material, has been stolen by using a popular Web resource called Copyscape (found at **www.copyscape.com**). When you go to Copyscape.com, you simply have to plug in your URL, and Copyscape will search the Internet to determine whether your content is being used elsewhere. The process generally takes only a few minutes.

Should you discover another individual or business is using content to which you hold the copyright, you should immediately contact the Web master via e-mail or by using whatever contact information is available, informing him he is infringing on your copyright and demanding that he take the stolen content down. If he fails to remove the content, you should immediately contact his Internet Service Provider. Internet Service Providers take copyright infringement seriously and generally will shut down the Web sites of anyone caught infringing copyright.

Will You Need a Patent for Your Product(s)?

If you will be offering a product or products that you have personally invented, will you need to apply for a patent with the United States Patent and Trademark Office to protect your product?

Before you go any further, you must know what is eligible for a patent and what is not. According to the United States Patent and Trademark Office, the following types of products are eligible for a patent: "process, machine, article of manufacture, composition of matter," or an improvement on any of the preceding.

That which cannot be patented, according to the USPTO, are "laws of nature; physical phenomena; abstract ideas; and literary, dramatic, musical, and artistic works." Additionally, those products that are morally offensive and that are simply not useful are exempted from receiving a patent.

First, it is important to understand that, in addition to product inventions, you can patent business systems. Before you decide whether or not to begin the long, arduous, and expensive process of applying for a patent, you will want to know and understand what the process entails.

As a side note, while you can file a patent for a business system you may have implemented or invented, you may want to consider going a different route. Rather than applying for a patent, if you have a business system, you may want to consider offering a license that will allow other businesses to use your business system. In such an instance, you should consult a lawyer who will be able to draw up a contract detailing the financial and exact terms of the license for users.

Applying for and filing a patent request is a long and often expensive endeavor. However, if you have invented a product, consider filing for a patent once you have shared your product publicly.

United States' laws dictate that if you sell your invention, discuss it in a publication, or show it at a trade show, you have one year to apply for a patent. If you fail to apply for a patent in that time period, you can only do one of two things: You can forfeit your right to file the patent for your invention or you can apply for a provisional patent which will give you an extra year to raise the money you need for the patent.

The best way to proceed, when you decide you want to file for a patent, is to consult an attorney who specializes in patents and who can lead you through the process.

You can learn more about filing for a patent at the United States Patent and Trademark Office's Web site at **www.uspto.gov**.

5

BEFORE YOU OPEN

B y this point in the process, you have already made some major decisions about your Web-based business, including business structure, business name, what type of business you want to start (take your offline business online, startup, affiliate business, selling products with a drop shipper, or purchasing products from a wholesaler and selling them), and your niche.

Your next step is to begin gathering the equipment and software you will need to get your Web-based business up and running.

EQUIPMENT YOU WILL NEED

Fortunately, starting a Web-based business actually requires very little overhead, especially if you already have a computer and an Internet connection. Following is a list of the equipment you will need to launch your Web-based business.

Computer

Your computer will be the heart of your Web-based business, so make sure it is reliable. If you are like most people, you probably already have a computer. But if you do not or you want a separate computer for your business, decide what type of computer is best for your needs and shop around to find the best deal.

The first decision you will have to make when choosing what type of computer to buy is: desktop or laptop? Consider the following factors when deciding which will work best for your business needs:

- What is your budget? Desktop computers are generally far more affordable than laptops.

- How important is portability?

- What are the features you must have with your computer? Create a list. Your list may include: a certain size monitor, plenty of memory, and a fast processor.

- How big of a computer do you want? It may sound like an odd question, but if you are going to purchase a laptop, it is a valid consideration, especially if you will be working with the laptop resting on your lap. Some laptops are much bigger and heavier than others. You will find lightweight laptops, but you are going to pay much more than you would for a heavier laptop.

- How important are ergonomics to you? With desktop computers, you can purchase ergonomic keyboards that will make your typing experience more natural and more comfortable. You can also buy an external ergonomic keyboard or mouse for laptops.

Buying a computer — whether it is a desktop or a laptop — is a considerable business expense. Do not rush into your decision. Instead, take the time to research your options. Read reviews by industry publications (PC Magazine, for example) and by those who have purchased and used the computers you are considering.

Compile a list of your favorite computers, based on what you learned during your research. Even if you decide to purchase your computer online, go to a local computer store and test run the computers. Try out the keyboard —

is it comfortable for you? Do you like how the mouse works? (This is particularly important if you are looking at laptops — some laptops have a touchpad while others have a roller button. Some have both.) Use the mouse to determine if it is something with which you can easily work. Is the screen large enough for you? Is the screen resolution clear enough?

Once you have decided on the best computer for your needs and have test run the computer, you will be ready to purchase your computer. It is always best to shop around before you purchase your computer. Comparison shop online and in your local stores to find the best deal.

High-Speed Internet

Unless you live in a rural area where only a dial-up Internet connection is available, you will want to opt for high-speed Internet service, such as broadband, DSL, or cable. Regardless of what type of high-speed Internet service you use, you will need to ensure your connection is secure, so others cannot log onto your connection, which we will discuss in Chapter Eight, "Securing Your Web-Based Business."

A Web Site

Your Web site is your business card, your store front, and the heartbeat of your Web-based business. Some Web-based business owners opt to hire a Web designer to design their Web sites. However, if money is an issue early on, you can create your own Web site using free or inexpensive templates and a Web design program like Microsoft FrontPage or Dreamweaver. You may also be able to find a new, less established Web designer to create a site for you at a lower cost.

We will discuss building your Web site in Chapter Seven, "Designing Your Web Site."

Reliable Web Host

A reliable Web host is essential. You do not want your Web site to experience downtime. Downtime could very well cost you business. We will discuss the intricacies of choosing a Web host in Chapter Six, "Your Web Site."

E-mail Address

As a Web-based business owner, you never want to use a free e-mail account, such as Yahoo or Hotmail, for business correspondence. Rather, establish an e-mail account through your Web site (me@mybusiness.com, for example). Most Web hosts allow you to have unlimited e-mail addresses so you can have a specific e-mail address for all of your business needs, i.e. info@mybusiness.com or customerservice@mybusiness.com.

Assess Your Business Assets

Essentially when you assess your business assets you are assigning a value to them. By doing so, you will know what your business is worth, which will be valuable if you decide to sell your business in the future.

Your tangible business assets are those assets that are physical, such as your business furniture, computer, in-stock inventory, land, buildings, and equipment. To determine the value of your tangible assets, you will likely need to consult an appraiser.

Not all assets, however, are tangible. You will likely build a wealth of intangible assets, including brand recognition, a strong customer base, copyrights, trademarks, and long-term contracts. There are three ways you can assess your intangible business assets.

First, you can calculate how much it will cost another entrepreneur to create the same asset from scratch.

Second, you can research the market and find a business with comparable intangible assets and value it that way.

Finally, you can assess your intangible business assets by figuring out the benefits that will result from the business through profits or sales and how long it will take to make that income.

An appraiser will be able to help you determine how much your business is worth. However, make sure you choose an appraiser who has experience appraising both tangible and intangible assets.

Opening a Business Bank Account

Opening a small business bank account is an essential step to getting your business off the ground. Even if you are a sole proprietor, you will want to keep your business bank account separate from your personal bank account. Having a small business bank account is essential to showing your business's professionalism, to ensuring you have an accounting of what business expenses you have paid out, and to make it easier to keep track of your profits.

Research your small business banking options in your city or town. Some factors you will want to take into consideration include:

- Does the bank offer online banking for small businesses? Will you be able to access your account, check your account balance, view checks that have been paid out, and keep track of your expenses?

- Is the bank local or are there branches available nationally?

- What fees are there for opening and/or maintaining a small business account?

Generally, when you open a small business bank account, you will need to present documentation, such as your EIN number. Ask the banks exactly what information they need for the process.

ACCOUNTING CONSIDERATIONS

How to Budget for the Expenses for Starting Your Business

Creating a budget is essential to your eventual business success. A budget allows you to determine what expenses you will have to cover each month, and it also helps you prepare for any unexpected expenses.

When you develop your budget, you will start by asking yourself the following questions:

- How much capital will you need for the necessary equipment to run your business?

- How much capital will you need for help (i.e. employees or independent contractors)?

- What are your total expected startup costs?

- What is your expected profit?

- How much money will you need for your day-to-day costs?

- How much revenue will you need to keep your Web-based business up and running?

It is critical that you answer each of these questions to determine whether you can make enough money to meet each of these needs. For example, you may not be able to make enough profit to hire an employee in the beginning. If you take the time to answer the questions, you will know that. If you do not do so, you may well hire an employee and find yourself struggling financially as a result.

If you have discovered your expected revenues will not be enough to cover all of your costs, start cutting back. That may mean not hiring an employee at the outset or not purchasing a top of the line computer. Make the cuts now, so you do not suffer later on.

The good news is your Web-based business's budget does not have to be complicated; you can keep it simple. The Better Business Bureau suggests starting with only two pieces of paper. Title the first page "Income" and the second page "Expenses." List all your projected income for the following year.

You also want to list all of your expected expenses for the next twelve months. There are two types of expenses you will have to take into consideration: fixed expenses and variable expenses.

Fixed expenses are the expenses you will have every month, such as rent (if you rent an office), utilities, and insurance. Variable expenses, on the other hand, are not set and are likely to fluctuate. Among the variable expenses you may have are advertising costs, taxes, and maintenance and repair to your business equipment.

The Better Business Bureau warns small business owners that there are several common mistakes that should be understood and avoided. First, ensure your budget is realistic. Be reasonable about your projected income and your expected expenses. Sure, you want to be optimistic about your first year in business, but do not get cocky. Otherwise, your business may suffer from a lack of funds.

You also want to include all of your taxes – local, state, federal, and sales taxes, if applicable – in your budget. Failure to include taxes in your projections will only come back to haunt you at the end of the year.

Finally, even though you want to keep your budget simple, make sure you include enough details so that you are easily able to keep track of your cash flow, your working capital, and your production costs.

Bookkeeping

As a small business owner, you must stay on top of your accounting. You may want to do all of your business's bookkeeping yourself or you may want to hire an independent contractor or an employee to do it for you. There are several ways to make your bookkeeping much easier, including:

- *Keep daily records.* Write down the money that comes into your business and goes out of your business on a daily basis. Get into a routine of daily record keeping and stick to it.

- *Keep careful records of checks you use and void.* Keep track of your checks, logging what each is used for and those that you have voided. At the end of the month, after you have received your canceled checks back from the bank, go through each one to make sure it matches with your records.

- *Find a good accounting program.* As we will discuss in the next section, there are a variety of accounting programs that can help you keep track of your business's finances. The key is to find one that works for you and your business.

- *Pay attention to your bank account statements.* Compare your bank statements at the end of each month to the financial records you have kept. By comparing the two, you will have an easier time reconciling where your money has gone, and you will be better able to track your expenses.

- *Keep strong records, in case of an audit.* Keeping impeccable records will also help in case you are audited by the IRS. That means you should be able to track every financial transaction and every invoice you have sent. To determine if your records are effective, go back and reconstruct the finances of your Web-based business for the previous year. Are there jumps in check numbers or invoices? (You should always use checks and send invoices in numerical order.) Can you track your financial records? If you can, your bookkeeping is effective. If you cannot, reevaluate your record keeping and determine where you can do better.

- *Do not do it by hand – use a computer instead.* Long gone are the days of keeping records by hand and storing them in file cabinets. Everything is done on computer today, and your bookkeeping should be no exception. Always remember to back up your computer records, so if your computer crashes or something happens that causes you to lose everything on your hard drive, you have another copy of your important information.

Accounting Software Overview

As a Web-based business owner, you are going to need to keep careful track of where your business money is going for tax purposes. The good news is you do not have to be a math wizard to keep your accounting in top shape.

Some of the most popular software used for small business accounting are QuickBooks, Corel's Quattro Pro, Microsoft's Excel, and Peachtree. You will want to find and use an accounting program with which you are comfortable.

- **QuickBooks** – QuickBooks is available for both Windows and Mac users and is available in several versions ranging from the basic QuickBooks Simple Start, which allows you to track your expenses and sales easily and effectively, to QuickBooks Pro, which allows you to create your own reports and invoices. You can learn more about QuickBooks by visiting them on the Web at **quickbooks.intuit.com/**.

- **Quattro Pro** – A Corel program, Quattro Pro is Corel's equivalent of Microsoft's Excel. (Interestingly, Microsoft offers a file conversion tool for those who want to transfer their Quattro Pro data to Excel.) Quattro Pro allows users to create simple and complex spreadsheets; import delimited text files; use visible tracking of editing in workbooks; and the ability to publish your workbook in either HTML or XML. Quattro Pro is part of Corel's WordPerfect Office Suite. Corel is located on the Web at **www.corel.com**.

- **Excel** – Packaged with Microsoft Office, Excel is a popular spreadsheet program that allows you to create both simple and complex spreadsheets. Features of Excel include the ability to format cells and tables; to create massive spreadsheets, with a maximum of one million rows and 16,000 columns allowed; create mathematical formulas for easy computation; and create charts. You can learn more about Excel on the Web at **www.microsoft.com**.

- Peachtree – Peachtree Accounting offers a beginner's package, Peachtree First Accounting, which will help you make the transition to computerized accounting. Peachtree allows multiple users; allows for exporting of information to Excel; and provides an audit trail. You can try a free trial of Peachtree Accounting at **www.peachtree.com**.

Regardless of what type of accounting software you use, or if you decide to do all of your accounting by longhand, you must be vigilant and stay on top of your accounting. Keep track of your sales, customer payments, your expenses, and your income. If you fail to do so, you will find yourself running around and trying to piece together all your financial information when tax season rolls around.

Monthly Profit and Loss Statements

Your monthly profit and loss statement is critical to the future of your Web-based business. It is a planning and management tool that allows you to set financial goals for your business. In essence, a profit and loss statement will allow you to see all of the income and finances your business makes in a month or in a year, which, in turn, will allow you to develop a profit plan.

SCORE recommends that business owners have two profit and loss statement sheets. One sheet will contain your estimates, and you will complete the other sheet at the end of one month. You can then compare the two sheets to determine how close your actual expenses and income were to your estimates.

Your profit and loss statement will include the following categories:

- **Revenue**. Your revenue is your total net sales for the total items, of your products or services, sold. If you are estimating your revenue, estimate the total number of items, at the price you will set, you think you will sell each month.

- **Cost of Sales**. If you are selling a product, your cost of sales is simply how many products in your inventory you have sold in a given month. In addition to the actual product, your cost of sales may also include how much it cost you to purchase the product you sell, the cost of manufacturing the product, and the cost of packaging the product for shipping.

  If you are selling a service, your cost of sales is simply what it costs to provide your service(s) in addition to labor and materials.

To determine your total net sales, add the cost of sales for your product(s) or service(s).

- **Gross Profit.** To determine your gross profit, take the total cost of sales and subtract them from your total net sales.

- **Gross Profit Margin.** Divide your gross profit by your total net sales, and you will have the percentage of your gross profit margin.

- **Controllable Expenses.** Controllable expenses are those expenses that will fluctuate depending on factors such as the volume of your sales. Controllable expenses include such things as employee salaries or hourly wages, including any overtime, benefits (social security, health insurance, unemployment insurance, etc.), accounting and/or legal services, advertising, repairs and maintenance, taxes, utilities, office supplies, and dues and/or subscriptions.

- **Fixed Expenses.** Fixed expenses are those expenses that you will have every month, regardless of whether your business is booming or barely making money. Among the fixed expenses you may incur are: rent, utilities, insurance, business licenses and permits, loan payments, depreciation of business assets, and miscellaneous expenses.

- **Net Profit before Taxes.** You can determine your net profit before taxes by subtracting your total expenses from your gross profit.

- **Taxes.** Taxes are the federal and state income taxes your Web-based business will pay.

- **Net Profit after Taxes.** Figure your net profits after taxes by taking your net profits after taxes and subtracting taxes from it.

- **Total for the Year**. To arrive at your annual total, add each of the column's monthly expenses. For example, add all 12 months' fixed expenses to arrive at your annual total. Do this for each column of your profit and loss statement.

To see a sample profit and loss statement, visit SCORE's Greater Knoxville Chapter's Web site at **www.scoreknox.org/library/profit.htm#form**.

Profit Planning

Developing a profit plan is essential for the success and growth of your business. A profit plan will allow you to estimate your business's sales and gross profits for a particular period (per quarter or annually, for example).

In developing your profit plan, or income statement, you will:

- **Evaluate your business.** Sit down and compare your profit plan to your actual costs and sales. Were your projections on the money? Close? Not even close?

- **Identify needs.** Your profit plan will also identify holes in your business. For example, your business may have skyrocketed but you only have one employee. After viewing your profit plan, you may determine you need to hire several more employees or rent a larger office space for your growing business team.

- **Pinpoint purchasing needs**. If you are selling more products, you may need to add an additional supplier. By identifying your purchase needs for the year ahead, you can appropriately stock up on your products.

- **Consider other needs.** If you find that you do not have enough financing for the year ahead, you can begin planning to find additional means of funding.

Among the advantages of taking the time to develop a profit plan are:

- You will be able to adequately budget for expenses.

- You will be forced to think and plan for the future of your Web-based business.

- You will have an easier time spotting future problems, which will allow you to tackle problems head on.

If you have never developed a profit plan, you may want to enlist the help of a business professional.

Audit Information

No one – neither a businessperson nor an individual – wants to face what has become known as the dreaded tax audit. Unfortunately, audits are a part of life, and your small business may well face an audit during its lifetime. During an audit, you are responsible for proving to the IRS that you have: 1. Fully reported all the income your small business received for the given tax year, and 2. You were entitled to all of the deductions, expenses, and credits you took.

The key to surviving an audit is to be prepared. You must keep good records of all the money that is coming in and going out of your business. The rule of thumb is to keep all records for seven years.

When you are informed that your Web-based business has been flagged for an audit, you can request a postponement, which some tax experts recommend, so you can thoroughly prepare for the audit. However, the IRS is legally obligated to undertake the audit within three years of the filing date of the tax return. There are two exceptions to this rule. Should the IRS determine that you have either committed tax fraud or if you have significantly underreported your small business's income, you will face an audit much sooner.

If you have not kept good records and are missing your receipts or other financial information, you should do your best to piece together that information for the IRS auditor. To avoid having to gather information after the fact, make it a habit to keep good records.

Give the auditor only the tax returns for the year that is being audited. Furthermore, you only want to supply the auditor with the information he requests; never offer information, and only bring that information that has been requested to the actual audit.

Experts recommend that you go to the IRS for the audit, rather than you inviting the auditor to your home or to your place of business to conduct the audit. Should the auditor request that the audit be held at either your home or business, contact your tax consultant. If you do not have one, get one and ask for his advice. You will also need the aid of a tax consultant should any mention of tax fraud arise.

Ultimately, you will probably have to pay some money to the IRS. After the audit, you will receive an examination report in the mail with the auditor's findings. If you disagree with the findings of the audit, you do have the option of appealing those findings. When you appeal an audit's findings, you file an appeal with the Tax Court or with the IRS.

Regardless of whether you are audited, you want to know your rights as a taxpayer. The IRS has published a free publication, "The Taxpayer Bill of Rights II," which gives you an in-depth look at your rights as a taxpayer. You can access the PDF report at the IRS Web site by going to **www.irs. gov/pub/irs-utl/doc7394.pdf**.

You can also read other publications regarding your rights as a taxpayer by going to **http://www.irs.gov/advocate/article/0,,id=98206,00. html**, where you will find links to numerous publications on the subject.

HOW AND WHEN DO YOU PAY FEDERAL AND STATE TAXES?

When you run your own business, you are responsible for paying your local, state, and federal taxes. How and when you pay your federal and state taxes largely depends on your Web-based business's business entity. According to the IRS, there are "four general types of business taxes: income tax, self-employment tax, employment taxes, and excise taxes."

Income Tax

Unless your business entity is a partnership, you are responsible for filing an income tax return each year you are in business. The actual income tax form you will need to fill out depends on your business entity and is as follows:

- **Sole Proprietorship** – Form 1040 and Schedule C or C-EZ

- **Partnership** – Form 1065 or Form 1040 and Schedule E (Check with your tax advisor to find out which forms you are legally required to file.)

- **Corporation** – Form 1120 or 1120A

- **S Corporation** – Form 1120S

- **LLC** – Form 1040 and Schedule C, E, or F or Form 1065 or Form 8832. See below for a detailed explanation.

LLCs differ from other entities. If you run an LLC as an individual, you would file Form 1040, either Schedule C, E, or F. However, if the LLC is run by a corporation, the income tax return form to be filed would be Form 1120 or 1120S.

If your Web-based business entity is an LLC with more than one member, according to the IRS, you would either file Form 1065 for partnerships or Form 8832 for a corporation.

Self-Employment Tax

Your self-employment taxes are actually to pay for your social security and Medicare taxes. You are responsible for paying a self-employment tax if you make net earnings of $400 or higher. You will also be responsible for paying self-employment taxes if you fall into such categories as an independent contractor. For a complete listing of who should file self-employment taxes, visit the IRS document "Self-Employment Tax" at **www.irs.gov/ businesses/small/article/0,,id=98846,00.html**.

The forms you will have to file for self-employment taxes also depend on your business entity:

- **Sole Proprietorship** – Schedule FE

- **Partnerships** – Form 1040 and Schedule SE

- **Corporation** – N/A

- **S Corporation** – N/A

Again, LLCs differ in paying self-employment tax. If the LLC has filed its income taxes under a 1040, Schedule C or F, then members of the LLC must pay self-employment taxes on all earnings. Alternately, if the LLC has filed its income taxes as a partnership, both members of the partnership are required to pay self-employment taxes on their part of the partnership earnings.

Employment Taxes

Businesses with employees must pay employment taxes, and as a business owner, you are required to pay social security, Medicare, Federal Unemployment Tax (FUTA), and Federal income tax.

- Sole Proprietorship – Form 940 8109 or Form 941 or 944

- Partnerships – Form 941 or Form 943 for farm employees

- Corporation – Form 941 or Form 943 for farm employees/Form 940 8109

- S Corporation – Form 941 or Form 943 for farm employees/ Form 940 8109

If you are running a LLC with employees, you will be responsible for withholding taxes for your employees. Employees generally have to file either Form W-2 or Form 1099. If you fail to withhold taxes from your employees' paychecks, you can be held legally liable provided you are the person who is supposed to make the payments.

Excise Taxes

The excise tax applies to only certain types of businesses. According to the IRS, those businesses that must pay excise taxes are those that:

- Manufacture or sell certain products

- Operate certain kinds of businesses

- Use various kinds of equipment, facilities, or products

- Receive payment for certain services

If your business is required to pay excise taxes, you will likely have to file the following forms:

- Form 720. Form 720 covers such taxes as environmental,

communication, air transportation, fuel, first retail sale of tractors, trailers, and heavy trucks, and manufacturer tax(es) on certain sales or uses of various items.

- Form 2290. Your business must file this form if you own any vehicles that holds a gross weight of up to and over 55,000 pounds.

- Form 730. You may have to file excise tax Form 730 if your business conducts lotteries or holds wagering pools or if your business accepts wagers.

- Form 11-C. Much like Form 730, Form 11-C is required if your business involves wagers. Form 11-C is an Occupational Tax and Registration Return for Wagering.

If you do not know how or when to file your taxes, you should consult an accountant or a professional tax consultant. Find a reputable tax consultant or accountant as soon as possible, so you know what taxes you have to pay and when you have to pay them, before your business even starts making a profit.

Furthermore, the IRS provides a complete "Small Business and Self-Employed One-Stop Resource" on its Web site (**www.irs.gov/businesses/ small/index.html**) where you can find small business forms and publications, a complete listing of those business expenses that qualify for deductions on your income tax returns, information on the standard mileage rates allowed for small businesses, and tax law changes that may be pertinent to your Web-based business.

What Expenses and Equipment are Eligible for Tax Deductions?

Keeping track of your Web-based business's expenses is vital to ensuring you benefit from tax deductions each year. Among the expenses and equipment that are eligible for tax deductions are:

- Office supplies

- Equipment – i.e. your computer, fax machine, copier, and scanner

- Computer software

- Mileage (when you are driving for business purposes)

- All your retirement contributions

- All business-related phone calls on your home phone

- A business phone line and its related charges

- Health insurance and health-related expenses (i.e. prescriptions)

You should also be aware of those expenses that are not deductible by law, including a home phone line, traffic tickets, and your clothes. The only situation in which your clothes are allowed to be deducted is if you must wear a uniform, something not pertinent for Web-based businesses.

If you are unsure of what expenses are tax deductible, ask yourself:

- Is the expense related to conducting of your Web-based business?

- Did you pay for the product or service during the tax year?

- Are your expenses both necessary and ordinary according to IRS guidelines?

Additionally, keep track of receipts for all your business expenses to make filing your tax return a much easier process and to ensure you receive all the deductions for which you are eligible.

You can learn more about those business expenses that are eligible for tax deductions by speaking to your accountant or by visiting the IRS's Web site at: **www.irs.gov/publications/p535/index.html**.

FINDING PRODUCTS

As we have already discussed briefly, you have to decide what products or professional services you are going to provide to your customers. Deciding which professional services you are going to offer will essentially come down to your skills. Finding products for your niche market, however, will likely take you more time and research.

Take three factors into consideration when deciding what products you are going to sell. First, are the products non-perishable? If you are going to be selling perishable items, such as food or flowers, you are going to have to take that into consideration in terms of both packaging and shipping to ensure they remain fresh during transit.

Second, how easy is it to ship the product(s) you have chosen? If you have chosen a bulky or delicate item, for example, you will need to charge your customers higher shipping costs. Alternately, if you are going to sell a product made of glass, you will have to make sure you package it properly (unless you use a drop shipper) to protect against damage.

Third, remember that the lighter the product, the less expensive the shipping will be for your customers. Finally, as was mentioned before, you want to ensure there is a demand for the product or products within your niche market.

There are numerous means, both online and offline, of finding products, including the following.

Drop shippers/Drop Shipping Directories

Even if you decide not to use a drop shipper, you can find ideas here for the types of products you may want to sell to your target market. You can generally find drop shipping directories online or at your local library.

Wholesalers/Wholesale Directories

As with drop shippers, wholesalers can be an excellent way to find the right products for your target market. If you are looking for wholesale directories, take a trip to your neighborhood library or university library.

Trade Shows

Trade shows are an excellent way to find the perfect products for your niche market. Remember, you need to have proof that you are running a business to gain entrance into trade shows.

In addition to finding possible products to sell at trade shows, you can meet vendors who sell those products and collect price sheets to help determine who sells the chosen products for the best price.

Local Shops and Businesses

Peruse shops and businesses in your neighborhood. You may come across a mom and pop shop, offering products perfect for your niche market, that has yet to take their business online. Offer to sell the products through your Web-based business. You can offer to directly purchase the product then resell it or offer to sell it and divide the profits between your business and the other business.

eBay

eBay is a popular marketplace for buyers and sellers around the world. You may also find it a useful place to find the products you want to sell. You may even be able to find wholesale products that you can purchase and then sell to your customers.

Area Crafters

You may not realize it, but your city or town is likely home to several talented crafters who produce unique and saleable products. If you find a product or products you like, find out if the crafter will give you a discount if you buy in bulk.

If the crafter does not agree to a discount, ask if he or she would be interested in selling his or her products through your Web-based business and dividing the profits with you.

Finally, if the premise of your Web-based business is to make profits through affiliate commissions, you are also going to need to research your product options online. There are literally thousands of online products available to affiliates.

Again, the key for you is to find those products that will appeal to your target market and that will provide you with the highest commissions. In some instances, you can find affiliate programs that pay as much as a 75 percent commission. Search for the ideal products with the best commission rates. Do not settle for a small commission, like 5 percent, when you can find quality products with affiliate programs offering as high as a 50 to 75 percent commission.

The best, and simplest, way to start your search for products offering affiliate programs is by visiting ClickBank (**www.clickbank.com**) or Commission Junction (**www.cj.com**).

CO-BRANDING

Co-branding is a very popular marketing tactic in the offline world. And although the concept has not yet received the same popularity online, this seems poised to change in the coming years. Regardless, co-branding is an important concept of which you should be aware as you move forward with your Web-based business.

Essentially, co-branding is when two businesses or companies join together to create a brand new product. There are endless opportunities for co-branding, especially in the offline world.

Co-branding first gained popularity in the 1980s when the popular Red Lobster chain opened restaurants in Holiday Inn hotels in Virginia and Arkansas. Since then co-branding has become a powerful marketing strategy.

Some popular and successful offline co-branding campaigns you have likely heard of include:

- Ford Explorer's special Eddie Bauer edition

- AT&T's Universal MasterCard

- Subway restaurants in Wal-Mart

- Taco Bell and Pizza Hut in a Sheetz gas station

Many online businesses are now realizing the many benefits of co-branding and are beginning to look for other businesses with which they can start a co-branding relationship. For example, the online chat and voice messenger, Skype, teamed with the dating Web site Verbdate. Members of Verbdate can download Skype for free and chat with other members for free whenever they see them online.

If you can find another business to team with, you will find that the advantages of co-branding are numerous. First, you have the opportunity to offer your customers a product or a service that is better than those already on the market. Other distinct advantages of co-branding include:

- Your customers will receive a greater value from your product or service than they will from your competitors' product or service.

- You will be able to improve your competitive position in the online marketplace.

- You will have the opportunity to broaden your customer base even more.

- If the co-branding is successful, you will reap the financial benefits with a higher profit margin.

If you decide that co-branding is an avenue you want to explore, you will need to find potential co-branding partners. You can start by researching other businesses. When you find a business you are interested in co-branding with, you should:

- Learn as much as you can and really get to know your potential co-branding partners. What type of track record do they have in the business world? How successful are they in penetrating the market?

- Find out how your potential co-branding partners operate their businesses.

- Ensure you have a contract written that defines the exact terms of your co-branding relationship.

Ultimately, co-branding can potentially expose your Web-based business to a larger market and garner you bigger profits, provided you find a suitable co-branding partner.

PRICING YOUR PRODUCTS

One of the most important decisions you must make is how to price your products or services. If you are purchasing your products directly from a wholesaler, you are likely getting the wholesale price. That means you can offer products to your customers at a lower price, if you choose, but remember that you also want to make a profit.

In some instances, those who sell products decide to simply use the manufacturer's suggested retail price. While you may find this is the easiest avenue to take, unfortunately, it may not be the best way to price your products. For example, if you go with the manufacturer's suggested retail price, you may find that the price does not work compared to the competition or it may inflate your price to a point where it pushes customers to your competitors.

There are several keys to effectively pricing your products or services. If you do not understand the market for your products or services, you are not going to be able to price them properly. Additionally, you need to know who your competition is and how much they are charging for the same or similar products or services.

The fact is you do not just do your research, set your prices, and forget about it. Your market will constantly be changing with new competitors entering and old competitors bowing out. There will be advances in technology that change the way you do business, and the market demand may rise or fall. It is critical that you are aware of each of these factors to ensure your pricing is still effective.

If you are selling a product or products, you are going to have to figure in your operating costs when setting your prices. Operating costs may include rent for your office space, supplies, utilities associated with running your Web-based business, wages you may pay to employees or independent contractors, the fees you pay to advertise your Web-based business, and business insurance.

Once you take into account the operating expenses and allow room for profit, you will determine your markup price. You can either express your markup in terms of dollars or in percentages. For example, if you have priced a product at $25 and your markup was 25 percent, the original cost of your product was $18.75.

If you are selling more than one product, you can do one of two things when determining markups. First, you can simply have a standard markup that is used for all your products. Or you can determine the markup for each product separately.

Going with a standard markup may seem like the simplest route to take, but is it the wisest? That is something you will have to decide for yourself, but consider this: You may have a product that sells very easily and therefore costs very little in advertising to get customers to buy, while you have another product that you pour your advertising budget into but still does not sell as well. The first product will likely yield a much higher profit than the second one. In fact, you may well lose money on the second product.

PRICING YOUR SERVICES

If you are going to be selling your services through your Web-based business, you should approach setting your prices a bit differently. In many instances, prices varying depending on experience. For example, let us say you are a Web designer and you are selling Web design services. If you are new to the industry, you will likely charge less than a Web designer with years of experience, an established reputation, and a strong portfolio. If you are that experienced Web designer, you are likely to charge much more than the new Web designer.

To start, do some research to determine the industry standard rates for the services you will be offering. Then you will need to consider the costs associated with the service you will be providing, including materials you may need to use, operating expenses, and labor. You will also want to take into account travel time.

Additionally, determine whether you charge per hour or per project or if you want to have both options depending on the client or the project. Your ultimate goal is to set prices that cover your overhead costs while also giving you a profit.

ESTABLISHING A RETURN POLICY

If you are selling a product, you are likely going to have to deal with customers who simply are not satisfied with the product they have purchased or who have changed their minds. You will have to answer the following questions when establishing your return policy:

- What type of return policy will you offer your customers?

- How long is a return policy for a full refund valid – a week, a month?

- Who will pay for the shipping for the product to be returned?

Some Web-based businesses, like the popular online bookseller **Alibris. com**, pay for the return shipping on orders that contain a mistake on the part of the company.

Make sure you have a written return policy that is outlined on your Web site and is on the receipt or the invoice you send to your customers, both with their packages and online.

DETERMINING SHIPPING RATES

If you are going to be selling a product directly to your customers, you need to determine your shipping rates. There are several things to take into consideration when setting your shipping rates.

Start by getting the shipping rates for several different shippers, including the U.S. Postal Service, FedEx, UPS, and DHL. Once you know what the shipping rates are for various companies, decide which shipper offers the best service for the best price.

After you have picked the shipper you want to work with, ask yourself two questions. First, how much will the packing materials themselves cost you? Second, what will be the cost of the shipping for your average orders?

Once you have answered those two questions, create a spreadsheet. On that spreadsheet, list the products that you're selling directly to your customers in one column. In another column, write the expected shipping price of each, which will allow you to estimate the shipping costs for various sizes of customers' orders.

Set your shipping rates so you will have room if the mailing rates increase. Your customers will expect to pay shipping when they purchase products online. However, you must ensure that the shipping does not raise the price of the product so high that your customers would be better off going to their local mall to purchase the same item. Do not send your customers to the competition because of soaring shipping costs.

When determining your shipping rates, consider whether you are going to offer standard shipping only or if you will also offer expedited and overnight shipping. Offering several shipping options will likely appeal to your customers, especially those who are in a hurry to have their orders delivered.

Finally, you may want to consider trying to negotiate for better shipping rates with the shipper you have chosen.

WHAT NOT TO DO

Starting a Web-based business means you will have low startup costs, unless you go the route of purchasing and selling from a wholesaler, in which case you will need money for your starting inventory. There are several things you should not do, at least in the beginning, when starting your Web-based business.

Do not hire employees. Hiring employees is a considerable expense. Even if you are hiring someone part-time, you have to take into consideration salary or hourly wages, taxes, Social Security, unemployment taxes, and other costs. If you hire someone full-time, you will have to consider a salary plus benefits or health insurance, which you may not be able to afford in the beginning.

If you need help in the beginning, consider using the services of an independent contractor. Independent contractors are freelancers who pay their own taxes and who work with clients on a contractual basis. You may use a freelancer for a day, a month, or even for longer, and best of all, freelancers can work from home.

Finding a freelancer is actually quite easy. You can either conduct a search online by plugging in "freelance writer" or whatever type of freelancer you need. If you are looking for a creative or legal freelancer, you will find there are numerous bidding Web sites online where you can likely find a freelancer for your needs.

The premise behind the bidding sites is simple: You post a project listing your needs, and service providers bid on your job. Experienced service providers have feedback and rankings – for example, four stars out of five stars. Read each provider's feedback carefully to ensure you choose someone with a strong track record. Some buyers prefer to work only with established providers while others will give new providers a chance.

Some of these types of sites claim they offer buyers a high quality product for very little. Keep in mind that you get what you pay for, and that is often the case with freelancers as well. However, some freelancers will work for less when they are just starting out.

Popular freelance bidding sites include:

- Elance – **www.elance.com**

- Guru – **www.guru.com**

- Rentacoder – **www.rentacoder.com**

- Ifreelance – **www.ifreelance.com**

Do not stock your own inventory. If you want to sell another company's products, use a drop shipper, at least at first. The reason for choosing a drop shipper rather than stocking your own inventory is simple: With a drop shipper, you do not have to order and pay for the product until the customer pays you. As such, you do not have to use money out-of-pocket, an expense you might not be able to afford as an upstart Web-based business.

However, if you stock inventory, you are stuck with it even if customers do not purchase the products, which means you are taking a financial risk.

Do not have a physical store or office location in the beginning. One of the biggest attractions of starting a Web-based business is the relatively low startup costs. Renting or purchasing an office or retail space is generally not a good idea when you first start your business. If you decide to rent or purchase an office or retail space, remember the other expenses you will have to pay, including utilities, insurance, and business licenses where warranted.

Wait until you grow your business and you are making a profit to determine if you really need and want the office and/or retail space.

6

YOUR WEB SITE

Your Web site is your virtual business card. It is going to define your business and may well be the first impression potential customers get of your business. But your Web site is more than your business card; it is an important tool that will set you apart from the competition. It is also the heart of your Web-based business.

Therefore, your Web site has to be as professional as possible. A poorly designed Web site reflects poorly upon your business and, subsequently, upon you. Your Web site is your virtual storefront, and you want it to be easy for your customers to navigate and purchase your products or services.

Before you can even think of designing your Web site, however, you must first choose and register your domain name and then find a reliable Web host. Shopping around and researching is vital during this process.

HOW TO CHOOSE A DOMAIN NAME

The first step in establishing your Web site is choosing your domain name. Your domain name is your address on the Web, and it is going to help you brand your business. Therefore, take time to decide what domain name will best serve your business needs.

Following are a few tips to keep in mind when choosing a domain name:

- Do not make your domain name too long. You are allowed up to 63 characters for your domain name, but even that is a bit lengthy. If your domain name is too long, people are going to have a much more difficult time remembering it. Keep your domain short and memorable.

- Make sure you are not infringing on another individual's or business's trademark.

- Decide which extension you want for your domain name - .com, .net., .org., .biz. or .info. You may want to register your domain name with several extensions, just so the competition cannot grab them. (It is not uncommon for businesses to purchase multiple extensions to keep them from the competition.)

- Consider buying several versions of your domain name; i.e. www. my-business.com or www.mybusiness.com. A great example of buying several domain names all pointed to one site is **www. flowers.com**. If you type **www.flowers.com** into your address bar, you will be taken to **1-800-Flowers.com**, a Web site that sells flowers, plants, teddy bears, and other gifts.

- Is your name one that can be easily misspelled? If it is, you should consider purchasing domains of common misspellings of your domain name. That way, if someone misspells your domain name when he or she types it in the address bar, he or she will still be rerouted to your Web site.

- Your domain name should be descriptive and should tell prospective clients what your business offers. For example, it is easy to tell that **www.CDnow.com** sells CDs. Prospective customers should know your business purpose just by looking at your domain name.

- Your domain name should be easy to remember. After you have decided on your domain name, you are going to have to purchase and register it with a domain registration company. There are a plethora of companies that allow you to register your domain name quickly and inexpensively. You must renew your domain name annually, unless you purchase a longer package.

The company with which you have registered your domain name will send you e-mail notices that your renewal date is approaching. In most cases, you can also allow for an automatic renewal, in which the host simply charges your credit card when renewal time comes around.

Make sure you do not let your domain registration expire, or another individual or business can snap it up. In fact, some domain names are so popular that people purchase them on backorder and buy them as soon as the original owner fails to reregister or decides not to reregister the name.

Some of the popular domain companies include:

- Domain Monger (**www.domainmonger.com**)

- Register.Com (**www.register.com**)

- Go Daddy (**www.godaddy.com**)

- Domain Bank, Inc. (**www.domainbank.net**)

- Yahoo Domains (**http://smallbusiness.yahoo.com/domains/**)

- Google Domains (**http://www.google.com/a/**)

You can also purchase your domain name when you buy your Web hosting. Before you register your domain name with a Web hosting company, however, make sure you know who is going to be listed as the registrant and legal owner of the domain name.

Many Web hosts offer complete packages that include both hosting and registering of the domain name. If the hosting package you are considering includes domain registration, contact the Web hosting company to confirm that you will be the legal owner of the domain name.

If the Web host is going to be listed as the registrant and legal owner, find another domain registrant and/or Web host. Having a Web host own your domain name may cause problems in the future. For example, the Web host may raise your annual registration rate, and you will have no recourse because you cannot transfer it to another domain registration company or Web hosting company because you do not own the domain. You will be at the mercy of the Web hosting company if you want to keep your domain name.

When you register your domain name, your contact information (including name, address, phone number, fax, and e-mail address) is going to become public information, unless you opt to have it remain private.

You can find out who owns a particular domain name by going to **www.whois.net** and typing in the domain name (without the www) and clicking on the correct extension. Once you do that, you will see a page that includes all of the contact information for the owner or owners of the domain name, provided the owner has not requested the information remain private.

Do not count on the fact that the domain name you want is going to be available with the extension that you want. There are several things you can do if the domain name you want is already taken. First, you can purchase the domain name with a different extension. Second, you can choose a new domain name and see if it is available instead.

Third, if you are set on having the exact domain name that is already registered, you can try contacting the owner of the domain, if the contact information is available on whois.net, ask if he or she is willing to sell the domain name, and if so, for what price. Obviously, you are not guaranteed the owner will be interested, but it is worth a try.

Finally, not all domains that are registered are actually in use and may be for sale. There are numerous domain brokers online who connect domain owners with domain buyers. For a cost, you may be able to purchase the domain name, with the extension, that you want. The cost of purchasing a domain through a broker can run into the hundreds, and even thousands, of dollars.

The popular domain brokers who may be able to help you include:

- Buy Domains (**www.buydomains.com**)

- After Nic (**www.afternic.com**)

- Impressive Domains (**www.impressivedomains.com**)

- Web Site Names (**www.websitenames.com**)

- Web Site Broker (**www.websitebroker.com**)

HOW TO CHOOSE A WEB HOST

Once you have decided on and registered your domain name, you need to find a reliable Web host. A Web host provides the server space on which your Web site will reside. There are literally hundreds of Web hosts from which to choose. Web hosting costs vary, depending on the host. In some cases, you can purchase your Web hosting annually, which can save you money.

There are also free Web hosts you can use, but steer clear of these if you want to present a professional image. First, you will not be able to have your own domain name. Instead of www.mybusiness.com, you will have something like www.freewebhost.mybusiness.com. Nothing says amateur like free Web hosting.

Second, free Web hosts can offer hosting for free because of the money they make from advertising. If you use a free Web host, your visitors are going to have to deal with advertisements all over the page, an annoyance and a tell-tale sign of an amateur. Using a free Web host may work if you are starting a Web site about a hobby or if you are using it as a place to upload your favorite photographs. But if you are a Web-based business owner, purchase your own Web hosting.

Before you begin your search for the right Web host for your business, you must decide what type of hosting you want. There are four types of Web hosting.

Shared or Virtual Hosting

Shared or virtual hosting simply means your Web site is being hosted on a server with the Web hosting company's other clients. Even though you maintain your own Web site, the hosting company manages the actual Web server. The upside to shared or virtual hosting is the relatively low cost. The downside is if another business's Web site is bombarded with visitors, it could slow down your Web site.

Collocated Hosting

When you go with a collocated host, you are responsible for buying the actual server, which you then give to the Web hosting company. In turn, the Web hosting company adds your server to its network. You maintain and support the server while the Web hosting company ensures the network is available for your server.

Managed Dedicated Hosting

When you use managed dedicated hosting, you actually lease the server from the Web hosting company. In turn, the Web hosting company maintains and supports the server, ensuring that security patches are updated; in addition, uptime is monitored, and the Web hosting company offers a warranty of hardware. Before you sign up for managed dedicated hosting, you must ensure the Web hosting company tells you exactly what managed services are included in the package. The downside to managed dedicated hosting is that some unscrupulous Web hosting companies try to pass off unmanaged dedicated hosting as managed dedicated hosting.

Unmanaged Dedicated Hosting

If you opt for unmanaged dedicated hosting, you will lease the server. Unmanaged dedicated hosting often means you will receive very little support, leaving you to monitor and manage the server yourself. As a Web-based business owner, you will probably be better off using managed dedicated hosting because you will receive more support. Unmanaged dedicated hosting typically runs about $99 a month.

Once you have determined the type of hosting you want, you are ready to start researching Web hosts. There are numerous factors you should take into consideration when choosing the best Web host for your needs:

1. The first thing you want to find out is if the Web host is capable of supporting e-commerce activities. If it cannot, move on to the next host.

2. Your Web hosting package should give you sufficient bandwidth, so that when you have a high volume of visitors to your Web site, they will not have to deal with pages that open slowly.

    In the simplest terms, bandwidth is the total amount of data that can be transferred over a network connection during a certain time period. Bandwidth is defined in terms of bits per second. If you have an Ethernet Internet connection, for example, you will have ten Mbps (ten million bits per second). The higher your bandwidth the more data can be transferred over the network per second.

3. Your Web host should offer you sufficient disk space. (Keep in mind that if your business grows to the point where you need more disk space, you can upgrade to a higher Web hosting package.)

4. Find out what type of connection speed the Web host uses. Some budget Web hosts run their servers on the 56K speed modems while the bigger Web hosts use the faster T1 or T3 high speed connections.

5. You want a Web host that will allow you to create e-mail addresses with your domain name, such as myname@mywebsite.com. Some Web hosts allow you to have an e-mail address with your Web host domain while giving you the ability to forward e-mails to your personal e-mail address. You also want to find out how many e-mail addresses you get with your Web hosting package. Can you purchase more e-mail addresses if you need them?

6. Ensure your Web host provides technical support 24 hours a day, seven days a week, by toll-free phone, live chat, or e-mail. When you run a Web-based business, you cannot afford to have a problem that will keep you offline.

    Also ask: Is the cost of the technical support the Web host provides included in your Web hosting package? Or do you have to pay extra for such support? Be sure to ask which types of support are not included.

7. Find out if the Web host performs backups periodically. If so, how often does the Web host perform them? Does the Web host have a backup server if the server your site is on goes down? How

frequently does the server go down? When the server goes down, how long does it take to get it up and running again?

8. Find out the typical uptime of the Web host's server. When you are looking at different Web hosts, you will likely come across a benefit that reads something like "99 Percent Uptime." If the Web host's site does not mention uptime, contact customer support to find out.

9. Make sure you will have enough POP addresses. Short for Post Office Protocol, POP e-mail addresses are simply your e-mail accounts and the protocols that ensure you can receive your e-mails.

10. Determine whether the host's server supports encryption. In non-technical terms, encryption puts your information in code and can only be read by the intended recipient. For example, you may offer your customers the option to pay for your products or services with a credit card. Encryption will ensure that the sensitive information will only be seen by you and your customer. Encryption also protects your e-mails, helping to ensure the e-mails are not intercepted by hackers.

11. Ask whether the server offers FTP. FTP, which stands for File Transfer Protocol, is an easy, convenient way to transfer files on the Internet. While you may not realize it, you likely use FTP all the time. Every time you download from the Internet – whether it is a song or a document – you are using FTP because you are transferring the file from another computer onto your computer.

12. Does the Web host provide tracking features? Tracking features allow you to monitor the traffic to your Web site, how your visitors arrived at the site, and exactly when they are on your

Web site. If the Web host does offer such a feature, ask exactly what the tracking feature entails.

13. Are you required to sign a contract? If you are, find out the specific details. How long is the contract valid? What happens if you are not happy with the Web hosting service and you want to cancel and move to another host? Is there a penalty for breaking the contract? If so, what is it?

14. What other features does the Web hosting package you are considering offer? Other available features you may need include:

   a. **Shopping cart.** A shopping cart allows your Web visitors to purchase products and pay for them directly from your Web site. The most popular shopping carts are PayPal, Agora, and OS Commerce. Some Web hosts offer several shopping carts while others offer only one.

   b. **Blog.** Blogs have become the newest Internet phenomenon, and they are a great marketing tool. While you can sign up for a free blog (i.e. **www.blogger.com** or **www.wordpress. com**), you will want your own blogging capabilities because it will be under your own domain name. For example, if you create a blog through your domain name, the URL will be www.mywebsite.com/blog. However, if you use a free blogging service, your URL will be www.mywebsite. blogspot.com. Having your own blog adds professionalism to your Web-based business.

   c. **Message boards.** Message boards can also be a valuable marketing tool, and many Web hosts make it easy for you to create and moderate your message board from your control panel.

d. **Design templates.** If you plan on designing your Web site on your own but do not know where to start, Web design templates can be invaluable. Many Web hosts offer FrontPage Web templates with their hosting packages. Design templates allow users to create Web sites step-by-step and require no knowledge of HTML.

e. **Chat room.** Another possible marketing tool, a chat room can provide your customers with a gathering place to share information and to chat.

Research different Web hosts before signing up with one. You want a Web host that provides strong customer support. Before you sign up, consider testing the customer and/or technical support of the Web hosts under consideration. Call the toll free number and open the live chat. How long do you have to wait for someone to help you? How friendly are customer and/or technical support? How helpful are customer and/or technical support? There is nothing worse than having a Web hosting problem and having to wait for an hour on the phone before getting sub par service. Take the time to research Web hosts now, so if and when you have a Web site emergency, you will get the support you need.

In addition to research, you may want to ask family and friends for any recommendations they may have. If they use a Web host, ask them about the uptime, the type of service, and if they are satisfied with the Web host's overall service.

You might also want to ask a Web host representative to provide you with testimonials from current clients. Furthermore, if you plan on checking reviews of different Web hosts, bear in mind that there are Web sites that review hosts simply as a money-making effort. For example, anyone can sign up to become an affiliate of most Web hosts. A popular way of getting affiliates signed up is for an individual to post positive reviews of each Web host with a link to the sign-up page.

Some popular Web hosts include:

- HostGator – **www.hostgator.com**

- GoDaddy – **www.godaddy.com**

- Ipower – **www.ipower.com**

- Yahoo – **www.yahoo.com**

- IX Web Hosting – **www.ixwebhosting.com**

- BlueHost – **www.bluehost.com**

- Lunarpages – **www.lunarpages.com**

- Start Logic – **www.startlogic.com**

- Easy CGI – **www.easycgi.com**

- Globat – **www.globat.com**

7

DESIGNING YOUR WEB SITE

Because your Web site is both your virtual storefront and your virtual calling card, you want to ensure it is as professional and as consumer-friendly as possible. Your Web-based business should always be open, 24 hours a day seven days a week, so your customers have the ability to purchase your products and services even while you are asleep.

The first step to designing your own Web site is researching the competition. Find out the type of Web site they have: What do you like about the competition's Web site? What works? What does not? Incorporate, in your own unique way, that which you like from the competitions' Web sites and avoid that which you do not like.

Know the Purpose of Your Web Site

First and foremost, you must know the purpose of your Web site or else it is destined for failure. Start by writing a mission statement. Ask yourself the following questions to help solidify your goals:

- What are your marketing goals for your business's Web site?

- Do you want your Web site to help you generate leads?

- Is one of your goals to create a list of e-mail addresses and phone numbers of potential customers?

- Will you offer customers an online catalog if you are planning to sell products?

Once you have started selling your products, you will want to add financial goals, such as increasing your sales by a particular sales percentage. As your Web-based business grows, you will likely need to modify your goals to suit the current situation.

Display Important Information Prominently

There is nothing more infuriating than going to a Web site and not being able to find contact information. You have probably experienced such frustration at least once.

For example, perhaps you have logged onto a phone carrier's Web site. You are hoping to find a customer service phone number. You do not see a "Contact Us" link on the front page, so you start clicking around. Five minutes later you finally stumble upon the phone number for which you are looking. By the time you pick up the phone to call customer service, you are frustrated and annoyed.

Finding contact information should not be difficult for your visitors. Some of them may very well give up instead of searching for the information if it is too difficult to find. Make it easy for them to access. Either have a link to your Contact Us page on every page of your Web site or have contact information (even if it is only an e-mail address) on each page of your Web site.

You should also provide your customers and potential customers with more than one way to get in touch with you: Display an e-mail address, a snail mail address, a phone number, and a fax number.

Failing to prominently display your contact information can lead to a loss of potential customers. Making it easy for your customers to contact you, and responding in a timely manner, are keys to building customer loyalty.

Make Use of Autoresponders

Autoresponders are an invaluable tool that you will want to use to help you promote your Web-based business and to respond immediately to your customers. Autoresponders are simply automatically generated e-mails that are sent when your customer performs a certain action on your Web site, such as e-mailing with a customer service question, signing up for product updates, or placing an order.

An autoresponder is your chance to impress your customers. Rather than your autoresponder being a simple message like "Thank you for ordering this product," be creative and offer your customers something valuable. Say, for example, that you have a newsletter that you send out to your customers on a monthly basis. When a customer signs up for your newsletter, set it up so an autoresponder is immediately sent to that customer confirming he has signed up for the newsletter.

The key to a successful autoresponder is to make it worthwhile for your customers. When your customer signs up for your newsletter, instead of writing a brief e-mail thanking him or her for joining, you might include a sample article from an earlier newsletter. Or you may want to send an entire newsletter to give the customer an idea of what to expect.

You also want to remember to include an opt-out link in every issue of your newsletter or for those on your mailing list.

Creating autoresponders is actually very easy. You simply have to log in to your Web site's control panel where you should find a link to the e-mail options.

Use CGI

Short for Common Gateway Interface, CGIs are essential for any Web site. CGI scripts allow you to receive forms your customers have filled out. For example, if you want your customers to have the ability to order directly from your Web site or to fill out and submit a Contact Us form, your Web host must allow CGI scripts.

To Use or Not to Use: Cookies

Cookies are both controversial and misunderstood. Those who are concerned about the security of their personal information and surfing habits set their Internet options to deny all cookies or to issue an alert each time they go to a site that uses cookies. If they still want to use the site, they allow the cookies.

Essentially, cookies are tiny text files that are put on your computer's hard drive by a Web site's server and are only viewable by the Web site that placed it on your hard drive. Cookies record information about your visit, such as your preferences and the specific pages you visited, making it easier for a Web site to customize its pages to your needs.

The downside to cookies is the misconception people have about their actual purpose. People have the mistaken belief that cookies expose them to viruses and are a type of spyware. Both are simply myths.

The upside to cookies is you can provide your customers with a personalized experience by keeping track of their preferences. If you want to see cookies in use, go to **Amazon.com.** If you already have an account with Amazon, you can log in to your account and purchase items by putting them in a shopping cart or you can sign into your account and shop with 1-click shopping.

With 1-click shopping, you simply sign in to your account, click on the 1-

click shopping, and your order is processed. Amazon stored your previous account information, using cookies, to allow you to have quick, one-click shopping when you returned to their Web site.

By using cookies, Amazon's 1-click shopping ensures you do not have to fill out your account information every time you purchase an item, saving you time and making purchasing from Amazon easy and convenient.

If you decide to use cookies on your Web site, you may want to tell your customers you are doing so and why. You may even want to consider writing a privacy statement in which you include a brief explanation as to what cookies are and how they will benefit your customers.

Considering Plug-ins?

In the simplest of terms, a plug-in is a program that allows Web site visitors to view multimedia and other content on a Web site. For example, if you use RealPlayer and QuickTime on your Web site, your visitors will need a plug-in to actually use the media player.

It is important to remember that not everyone has or wants plug-ins. Additionally, you must remember that not all of your customers are on broadband, cable, DSL, or another high-speed connection. Some are still using dial-up, either by choice or because there are no other options available where they live (i.e. rural areas).

There is actually an easy solution for dealing with plug-ins that will satisfy both those who have plug-ins and those who do not. You can offer two versions of your Web site: one for those with plug-ins and one in simple HTML. You have likely visited a Web site where the front page asks you to click on a link that will lead you to either a Flash site or an HTML site.

You can do the same thing or you can have your Web site designed to automatically detect whether your customer has plug-ins installed on his or her computer. If he does, he or she will automatically see the Flash version.

To ensure you cater to your entire customer base, consider offering two versions. Otherwise, you risk losing the business of those who do not have or do not want plug-ins.

Make Your Web Site Easy to Navigate

Your Web site must be easy to navigate or you are going to risk losing customers. Two of the most important and easy ways to keep your Web site consumer-friendly is to ensure you have a navigation bar prominently displayed on the side or the top of each page and to include a site map. Other ways to make your site navigable are:

- Include a search box. Give your customers the ease of searching for the product they're looking for by including a search box.

- Offer visitors an abundance of links. Links will help you and your customers. Provide your customers and potential customers with links to other sites that will offer them valuable information related to your niche. The more relevant links you provide, the better chance you will have of ranking higher in the search engines.

- If you have an online catalog or listing of merchandise available, make sure it is up-to-date. Do not wait until your customer is ready to check out to tell him or her the product he or she wants is currently sold out. That will only lead to frustration and could deter him or her from purchasing from you in the future.

- Be prepared to deal with service outages.

- Make sure you have an Application Service Provider (to help with payments).

- Ensure you have a Frequently Asked Questions (FAQ) page. A FAQ page will save you and your customers time. Anticipate what your customers' common questions will be and write and answer them in your FAQ section. As you are asked questions from numerous customers, you can add them to the FAQ section as well.

Web Site Taboos

As a Web user, you have probably come across more than one Web site feature that has annoyed or frustrated you, likely causing you to leave the Web site. Do not allow the same thing to happen to your Web site's visitors.

Rather, know those features that are Web site taboos, and avoid them at all costs:

- Not allowing users to hit the back button on their browser. You have likely been to a Web site where you have tried to click the back button to take you back to your search page, and no matter what you try, you cannot. So you are forced to restart your search all over again. If it is frustrating for you, imagine how frustrating it is going to be for your customers.

- Broken links. Make sure your links work. Clicking on dead links will annoy your customers. To ensure that links on your Web site are live, check them at least once a week. You may also want to have an e-mail link that customers can use to report a dead link if they happen to find one.

- Do not have the browser open into new windows every time

visitors click a link on your site. Doing so will only annoy your customers and slow their computer's response time. If they want to go back to the page they were visiting, they just have to click on the navigation bar.

- Information that is outdated should be avoided at all costs. You cannot simply publish your Web site and forget about it. You must keep it updated and accurate. For example, if you are selling products and one product is sold out, make sure you inform customers that the product is sold out before they get to the checkout phase.

- Not having a home page link on every page of your Web site. If you do not have a home page link on every page, how are people going to be able to go back to the home page if they want to?

- Avoid an overabundance of colors, fonts, and font sizes. Save that for your personal Web site. Your Web site should be consistent in its font type, size, and color. You should also avoid a black background. Most people are used to the white background of a Word document. Keep that in mind when you choose your color scheme.

- Avoid having too many graphics. Graphics can be a great addition to your Web site, if you do not overdo it. If your Web site has too many graphics, your visitors may experience long download times. If download times are too long, your customers may just leave the site instead. Remember, not everyone has high-speed Internet access, and downloading graphics can take considerable time, especially for those on dial-up.

- Avoid slow download times. Large or numerous graphics are not the only things that will slow down your Web site's download times. Media players, animation, and other online bells and whistles will contribute to a slower download. Take this into consideration when you determine how many fancy features you want on your Web site.

- Do not use a free Web host — it is simply unprofessional. Free Web hosts are great for personal Web sites, but if you are opening a bona fide Web-based business, you want people to take you seriously, and that means purchasing a domain name and Web hosting. The good news is Web hosting can be found for as little as ten dollars a month, an investment that will show your customers you are a professional.

- Do not use an "Under Construction" sign on your Web site. Rather than putting up an "Under Construction" page, let your domain remain parked. When you are ready to launch your Web site, simply publish it. An "Under Construction" page does not tell your potential customers anything. How long will your Web site be under construction?

- Sloppy grammar and editing. You want your customers to trust you, and an error-riddled Web site is a tell-tale sign of an amateur. Proofread all your Web copy to ensure it is accurate and there are no mistakes, even small ones. Your credibility depends on it.

- Do not inundate your Web site with ads. In today's online world, there are some Web sites that are designed specifically to create revenue with Google's AdWords. You do not want your Web site filled with ads – your aim is to earn revenue through selling your products or services.

Also keep in mind, as you proceed, that Web pages do not look the same in Internet Explorer as they do in Netscape Navigator, Firefox, or any other browser – another reason you want to keep your Web design as simple as possible.

While there may seem to be an abundance of Web site taboos, if you just eliminate these things from your site, you will ensure your customers have an easy, enjoyable experience, which means they will be more likely to return.

Your Web Site's Site Map

Once you have established your Web site's goals, map out your site and its pages. A site map helps your visitors easily navigate your Web site. Just as important, the site map will help ensure your Web site does not have too many or too few pages. You do not want to overwhelm your potential customers with unnecessary information, yet you also do not want your Web site to lack the information and pages it needs.

A basic Web site's site map can include:

- Homepage

- Contact Us page

- About Us page

- Page(s) listing products and/or services offered

- Testimonials

Your Web site may have more pages, but it should not have any fewer than those previously listed. Take the time to create your site map before you move any further with your Web site.

Your Web Site's Homepage

By now you should have a good idea what your Web site should and should not have. Now you want to consider what is actually going to go on the pages of your Web site. (We will discuss how to write compelling content in Chapter Ten, "Creating Powerful Content for Your Web Site.)

Your homepage is the most important page on your Web site. It is the first thing your visitors are going to see, and you have only seconds to grab their attention and keep them on the site.

Your homepage should contain some basic elements, on which you can build and add content:

1. First and foremost, your homepage must contain your Web-based business's name.

2. If you have a logo and/or a slogan, display them prominently on the homepage.

3. Display your contact information somewhere on the homepage. As we previously discussed, making contact information difficult to find is only going to frustrate your customers and may cause you to lose business.

4. You must have a navigation bar — either on the top or on the side of your homepage — so visitors know exactly what pages are contained in your Web site and easily navigate to them. Your navigation bar should be in the same place throughout your site.

5. Your homepage should also include a privacy statement or a link to your Web-based business's privacy statement. Before doing business with you, your potential customers want to know you are going to keep their personal information private and the steps you are going to take to protect their personal information.

6. Devote a section of your homepage to introducing new products and services to your customers. A "What's New" section is

popular on many Web sites and allows you to showcase your Web-based business's latest news.

Contact Us

As mentioned several times already, it is imperative that your customers can find your contact information. That means including a link to your Contact Us page and/or listing your contact information on every page.

And while your Contact Us page will be one of the most important pages of your Web site, it will also likely be the simplest page of your Web site. Make sure your Contact Us page includes your business name, business mailing address, telephone number, fax number, and e-mail address.

You may also want to include a form that customers can fill out and submit directly from your Web site. If you create a form, make sure you ask the customer for his e-mail address, phone number, and the best time to reach him or her. You will also want to have a box where the customer can write his or her question or comments before hitting submit.

About Us

Your Web site should include an About Us page, and the link should be included on your homepage. An About Us page is your opportunity to educate your potential customers about your business and your policies. You may also want to include a history of your business.

Products/Services

You will want separate pages for your products and/or services. For example, you may offer virtual assistant services to your clients. You may want to have a page for each of the different services you provide, as well as a detailed description of each. Alternately, you may find that a sole page for listing and describing your services is sufficient.

If you are selling products, you may want to include photos along with your descriptions and prices of each product.

Testimonials

When a customer is happy with your product or services, ask him or her if he or she would be willing to write a brief testimonial or give you a verbal testimonial that you can write down and then publish on your Web site. Testimonials are an excellent means of attesting to the quality of your product or service, customer service, and the quality of the purchasing experience you give your customers.

Designing Your Web Site

Should you design your own Web site or should you hire a professional to do it for you? Unfortunately, not all new Web-based business owners can afford to hire an experienced Web designer. Fortunately, however, there are affordable ways to design a professional Web site, even if you do not know HTML or other confusing Web design coding.

If you decide to design your own Web site, or to use a Web template to help you in designing your Web site, you will need to decide what Web design program you want to use. Several of the most popular Web design programs are Microsoft's FrontPage, Adobe Dreamweaver, Web Studio 4.0, Adobe GoLive, and Coffee Cup HTML Editor.

Some Web design programs include a free trial download so you can experiment with the software before deciding to purchase it. The key to finding the best Web design software for your needs is to research your options and test drive the software.

HTML

Short for Hyper Text Markup Language, HTML is simply the software language of the World Wide Web. If you do not know HTML, you can still design a professional Web site using Web design programs. However, basic HTML is not difficult to learn, and you can find numerous books online or in your local libraries or bookstores that explain how to use HTML in an easy-to-understand language.

Microsoft FrontPage

If you use Microsoft Office, you will likely find that using Microsoft FrontPage is rather easy once you get the hang of it. In fact, you do not need to know any HTML to effectively use FrontPage.

FrontPage gives you the ability to use either HTML or a blank screen, very much like a Microsoft Word Document, where you can drop in your own content and graphics and design your site using the available toolbars. If you know how to use Microsoft Word, you will likely become quickly accustomed to FrontPage.

Before you publish your Web site, you can preview it in a number of different browsers so you can ensure it looks cohesive.

While FrontPage offers its own templates, you can also find a plethora of templates, created specifically for FrontPage, from Web designers online. You can learn more about FrontPage by visiting Microsoft's Web site at **office.microsoft.com/en-us/frontpage/FX100743231033.aspx**.

Dreamweaver

Designing a Web site is more than putting some words and maybe some graphics into a Web page and publishing it. You have to take a lot into consideration before you begin the design process. Dreamweaver is another popular program that allows you to design and publish your own Web site.

Produced by Adobe, Dreamweaver allows designers, even those who are not fluent in HTML coding, to create their own Web sites. Like Microsoft FrontPage, you can either create your Web site in code or you can use a blank page and create it visually. Dreamweaver also allows you to easily add video and to preview your Web site in various browsers.

You can run through a Dreamweaver demo to determine if it is a program you would like to work with by visiting Adobe's Web site at **www.adobe. com/products/dreamweaver/**.

Web Studio 4.0

Another popular Web design program, Web Studio 4.0, allows you to design either in code or visually (like FrontPage and Dreamweaver). Among the more advanced options, Web Studio 4.0 offers designers compatibility with the latest version of Internet Explorer (IE7), flash slide shows, and drag and drop PayPal shopping carts.

Web Studio 4.0 is on the Web at **www.webstudio.com**, where you can sign up for a free 30-day trial download. The download allows designers to test drive Web Studio 4.0's software and enjoy free hosting to preview their Web sites.

Adobe GoLive

Like Dreamweaver, GoLive is a product of software powerhouse Adobe. (Dreamweaver was previously owned by Macromedia, but Adobe acquired the popular Web design software.) Adobe GoLive allows designers to design their Web sites either visually or by using code, and the software allows for drag and dropping, CSS, PHP, JavaScript, and XHTML. Adobe GoLive can be purchased as part of Adobe's Creative Suite or individually at **www. adobe.com/products/golive/**.

Coffee Cup HTML Editor

Like Dreamweaver, FrontPage, and Web Studio 4.0, Coffee Cup HTML Editor also allows you to design your site either with a code editor or a visual editor. One of the most affordable Web design programs, Coffee Cup HTML Editor is ideal for both new designers and more advanced designers. It also supports XHTML, CSS, and PHP. To download the free 30-day trial of Coffee Cup HTML Editor, visit **www.coffeecup.com/ html-editor/**.

USING A TEMPLATE

If you do not have the experience or the interest in designing your Web site from scratch, you can either find a free template or purchase a template. Templates allow Web design novices to easily create a professional-looking Web site rather quickly.

Unless you purchase full rights to a Web template (which can run several thousands of dollars), you should know that others will be able to purchase and use the same Web template as you. However, the Web is a huge place, and that should not pose a problem.

In some instances, those who offer free or cheaper templates require that you identify that the template is their creation, and you must link back to their Web site. Rest assured, however, that is not the case with all templates.

If you opt for a template, make sure you determine if the template is compatible with your Web design software. If you are looking for a FrontPage template, do a search for "FrontPage templates." The same goes for whatever software you are using.

Ultimately, using a template is an easy, convenient way to get your Web-based business's Web site online. And you can always hire a professional

Web designer to redesign your Web site once your business is up and running and making profits.

HIRING A PROFESSIONAL WEB DESIGNER

Hiring a professional Web designer does not have to be a stressful process, but you should be thorough in your search to ensure you choose the best Web designer for your needs and your budget. To start your search for the right Web designer, talk with family and friends and ask if they can recommend a reputable Web designer.

If you want a local Web designer, you may want to check in your local phone book under "Web Designers." Or you may want to visit your local Chamber of Commerce Web site where you can search for Chamber members that offer Web design.

You can also find Web designers on various Web sites that allow you to post projects and have service providers bid on those projects. If you decide to use a bidding site, make sure you evaluate each service provider, including the service provider's feedback and portfolio. You can find Web designers at such bidding sites as:

- Guru – **www.guru.com**

- Elance – **www.elance.com**

- Rentacoder – **www.rentacoder.com**

- Scriptlance – **www.scriptlance.com**

- Get A Freelancer – **www.getafreelancer.com**

- Project 4 Hire – **www.project4hire.com**

Once you find potential Web designers, evaluate who is right for your particular needs. Make sure each potential Web designer provides you with a link to his or her portfolio or links to Web sites he or she has designed.

You also want to ask potential Web designers to provide you with references of previous clients. Talking with references is an excellent way to gauge whether or not the previous clients were happy with the Web designer's work, customer service, and whether or not the Web designer completed the project satisfactorily by the designated deadline.

After you find a Web designer with whom you want to work, make sure you have a contract written that stipulates exactly what the Web designer is going to do for you, including:

- **Project specifications:** Exactly what is the Web designer going to do? Make sure the contract specifies whether or not the Web designer will also provide the Web site's content and what type of graphics will be used.

- **Deadlines:** State the start date of the project and list milestone dates, such as when the Web designer will provide you with a first draft. Also list the firm deadline for completion of the Web site.

- **Other conditions:** Will you or will the Web designer own your Web site's design? How many revisions are offered in the initial cost? If you need revisions beyond those quoted in the initial cost, what is the cost of each additional revision? What type of confidentiality is required of the Web designer: Will you allow him or her to use your Web site link in his or her portfolio? If not, make sure your contract states that, and consider having the Web designer sign a confidentiality agreement. Add any additional conditions that you want included in the contract.

- **Payment:** Include all payment dates, including date of deposit, milestone payment dates, and the date of the final payment. You should not release the final payment until your Web site is completed and you are satisfied with the final product.

You also want to make sure any graphics you use are not copyrighted by another individual or company. If you use copyrighted photographs, you can be subject to financial penalties. Ask your Web designer to show you who owns the copyrights to any graphics or photos he or she is using. There is an abundance of stock photos online that can be purchased for use on Web sites, but it is against the law to use photographs and graphics that are copyrighted without the consent of the copyright holder.

You must also consider who is going to update your Web site. Is that a service you want your Web designer to provide? If so, can you afford the monthly cost of updating? Or do you want the ability to update the Web site yourself? If so, make sure the program your Web designer uses to design the Web site is compatible with the Web-building program (i.e. FrontPage) you use.

If money is tight and you are not sure you can afford a professional Web designer, consider finding a Web design student who is willing to work for less pay and a great reference. You can ask friends, family, and co-workers if they know any college students studying Web design or your can contact your local community colleges and universities.

8

SECURING YOUR WEB-BASED BUSINESS

Whether you realize it or not, your Web-based business faces a variety of outside risks that can threaten the stability of your business, from theft or a natural disaster to hackers.

It is absolutely essential that you protect yourself and your Web-based business by knowing what risks you face and by taking action against those risks.

BUSINESS INSURANCE

Your Web site is the heart of your online business, but without your equipment — including your computer and your software — you are not going to be able to effectively run your Web-based business. That is why it is extremely important that you insure all of your important business equipment and office furnishings. If you have ever dealt with a computer, you know that things can go wrong: Your hard drive can inexplicably die, for example, destroying all your customer information and hard work. But there are also unexpected disasters, such as flood or fire, from which you need to protect your computer, other work equipment, and office furnishings. (Remember, because disaster can strike at any time, you must backup all your work on your computer frequently.)

You must protect your business equipment and office furnishings against natural disasters. If a tornado rips through your town and destroys your office, for example, your insurance will help you purchase new equipment. If you do not have insurance to cover your business, you are likely going to have to pay thousands of dollars to get your business up and running again.

But insurance protects you against occurrences you may never have considered. For example, will you have information and packages shipped to your business? What happens if the mailman or delivery person falls and injures himself or herself? Are you protected against such accidents?

Insurance protects you against the unexpected. If you are operating your Web-based business out of your home, you may believe that your homeowner's or renter's insurance will protect you and your business. But do you know for certain that such incidents are covered?

Your first step is to talk with your insurance agent to find out exactly what your homeowner's or renter's insurance covers. If it does not cover your small business, talk with your insurance agent and detail exactly what your Web-based business does and your business operations to determine if you can add your business to your already-existing policy.

There are several types of insurance you want to consider for your Web-based business: business equipment and furnishing insurance, automobile insurance, liability insurance, professional liability insurance, and workers' compensation.

Business Equipment and Furnishing Insurance

Your priority when dealing with insurance that covers your business equipment and office furnishings is ensuring that your insurance provides the full replacement cost of everything that is lost. There is a considerable monetary difference between insurance that offers you the full replacement cost and insurance that pays only for the used value of that which you have lost.

Automobile Insurance

Because you are running a Web-based business, you are likely not going to purchase a vehicle to use specifically for your business needs. If you are using your personal car or truck, make sure your automobile insurance covers you when you are using the car for business purposes.

If you hire employees, ensure they have adequate insurance if they will be using their vehicles for business purposes.

Liability Insurance

You must protect yourself against accidents that happen at your home but that are related to your business. For example, one of your employees or independent contractors may come to your home office for a meeting and somehow falls and hurts himself or herself. Such an incident will not be covered by your homeowner's or renter's insurance. However, your business liability insurance will cover such an occurrence.

Even if you do not have employees, you need liability insurance. If a delivery man hurts himself or herself delivering business supplies, your liability insurance will kick in and cover the injuries.

Professional Liability Insurance

Professional liability insurance, or errors and omission insurance, is relevant to those business owners who are offering professional services. Your professional liability insurance will protect you against lawsuits that claim you have made an error or an omission in the work you have conducted for your clients.

Product Liability Insurance

If you are going to be selling products that have the potential for injuring customers or for causing damage, invest in product liability insurance. Product liability insurance covers such occurrences as breach of warranty, negligence, and strict liability. Such suits can be filed against you, as the seller of such a product, or against the product's manufacturer.

To determine whether your business needs product liability insurance, talk with an attorney.

Workers' Compensation Insurance

While you may not have employees in the startup phase of your business, you may well need them in the future. The only state in the United States that does not require businesses with employees to have workers' compensation insurance is Texas. In other states, those small businesses with less than five employees are not required to purchase workers' compensation insurance.

Check with your particular state to find out what the rules are. Some states allow businesses to self-insure themselves in place of workers' compensation. So, in case of an accident or an injury, your insurance will cover the costs.

Your best bet is to know what your state's requirements are in regards to workers' compensation before you hire an employee. Knowing what to expect will help you anticipate costs associated with hiring employees.

INVEST IN ANTI-VIRUS PROTECTION

If your computer has ever been hit with a virus, a Trojan, or spyware, you know just how frustrating it can be to try to regain control over your system. As long as your computer is hooked to the Internet, it is vulnerable to viruses and other infiltrations. As a business owner, you must invest in some type of anti-virus software. Otherwise, you are exposing your business and your customers' personal information to unknown predators.

Many computers today come equipped with complimentary anti-virus programs that generally offer a few months of free service. When that service runs out, you will need to upgrade or purchase other anti-virus software. Below we will discuss some of the most popular anti-virus software programs available today. First, however, there are several terms with which you should be familiar.

Internet Virus

In its simplest terms, an Internet virus is a program that self-replicates itself and is spread from computer to computer through executable (.exe) files and other types of documents. Internet viruses hide themselves in other programs, making it easy for them to spread extremely fast.

An Internet virus may corrupt, and at the very worst delete, your computer's programs or system files. You will likely recognize the symptoms of a virus very soon after it attaches itself to your computer. If you notice your programs do not work as they should or you are unable to perform normal functions, your computer may have been infected and the critical system files may have been deleted.

Internet viruses are often sent through e-mail attachments. If you do not have anti-virus software that scans all incoming attachments, do not open any attachments from senders you do not know.

Spyware

Much like the name implies, spyware is software that is attached to your computer, without your consent or your knowledge, to "spy" on your Internet activities for advertising purposes. Those who want to track your Internet activities offer free downloads. When you initiate the free download, you also unwittingly have the spyware attached to your computer.

Adware

According to Microsoft, adware is "advertising that is integrated into software. Adware is often combined with a host application that is provided at no charge as long as the user agrees to accept the adware."

A host application, for example, may offer users the ability to automatically fill in their information when filling out Web forms. In exchange, the Web site offering the host application places adware onto the user's computer to monitor Web site usage and display pop-up ads.

Trojan Horse

Trojan horses are often attached to seemingly harmless programs. In reality, the programs contain the dangerous Trojan horse. A Trojan horse is a program with harmful or deliberately malicious code designed to damage your computer. Damage may include destruction of your hard drive or programs. Trojan horses are similar to Internet viruses; however, they do not replicate themselves.

Worm

Like a virus, a worm is a self-replicating program that contains malicious data that can shut down a computer or may consume your computer's resources, such as bandwidth. Unlike a virus, a worm is self-contained, which means it replicates itself without attaching to a program.

Norton Anti-Virus Internet Security

One of the most well known and popular anti-virus software programs is Norton Anti-Virus Internet Security. Norton scans all incoming and outgoing e-mail messages for Trojan horses, e-mail viruses, and SMTP worms. If an infection is discovered, the software automatically repairs the infected files.

Created by Symantec, Norton also includes adware and spyware detection tools. Among Norton's other features are: automatic updating of software, immediate scanning for viruses after downloading updates, automatic subscription renewal, and automatic cleansing by disinfecting your computer prior installing software.

If you have questions or need help using the software, you can e-mail Norton, use their FAQ page, or visit their help page. Unfortunately, phone support is only available to those who have purchased phone support. Subscribers can purchase annual subscriptions to Norton Anti-Virus.

You can learn more about Norton Anti-Virus by visiting its Web page at **www.symantec.com/home_homeoffice/products/overview.jsp?pcid=is &pvid=nav2006**.

McAfee's Anti-Virus Software: Virus Scan

Another popular anti-virus program is McAfee's Virus Scan, which protects computers from viruses, worms, Trojan horses, malicious Active X controls, Java applets, spyware, and adware. Updates to the software are downloaded automatically, so you do not have to worry about forgetting to download updates thus compromising your computer's security.

Perhaps the best part of McAfee's Virus Scan is the fact that it employs an Emergency Response Team that constantly monitors new threats, allowing them to take quick action and provide users with frequent software updates.

Customers with subscriptions to McAfee's Virus Scan can communicate with technical support via e-mail, help documentation, or phone. To learn more about McAfee's Virus Scan, visit the company's Web site at **www. mcafee.com/us/**.

AVG Internet Security

AVG Internet Security, made by Grisoft, is another leading provider of anti-virus software. AVG Internet Security protects computers from viruses, worms, Trojan horses, adware, spyware, and spam. Computer users can purchase subscriptions annually or for two years, and one subscription is valid for one computer. However, you can purchase licensing to use AVG Internet Security on up to five computers.

Grisoft offers free technical support for those customers who have registered for their product, but technical support is only available via e-mail. There is also an in-depth FAQ page. For more information about Grisoft's AVG Internet Security software, visit their Web site at **www.grisoft.com** and click on products.

Windows Live OneCare

Touted as the "all-in-one, always-on PC Care Service," Microsoft's Windows Live OneCare offers protection against viruses, worms, Trojan horses, phishing, and hackers. Users can scan individual files and folders for potential threats. It also periodically backs up your files, and updates are automatic.

Annual subscriptions are available, and one subscription can be used on as many as three computers. Microsoft provides technical support for subscribers online, 24/7. Windows Live OneCare offers a free 90-day trial. You can learn more about Windows Live OneCare or download the free trail at Microsoft's Web site: **onecare.live.com/standard/en-us/default.htm**.

Spybot

While generally not considered as thorough or as effective as other software because it focuses only on spyware, Spybot is a free program that scans users' computers for spyware and eliminates threats.

Among the type of spyware Spybot detects and eliminates are: Cydoor, File Freedom, Spyware Nuker, Spyware Installer, Speed Delivery, and Alexa-related spyware.

You can find and download Spybot for free at **www.spybot.info.**

THE FEAR OF INTERNET FRAUD

For your Web-based business to become and remain a success, you must build a relationship of trust and loyalty with your customers. With the threat of identity theft and fears of stolen private information, customers are wary about to whom they hand their personal information. And there is little wonder why. The statistics are staggering.

In 2005 alone, the Internet Crime Complaint Center received 231,493 complaints about Internet fraud, an increase of over 11 percent from 2004. Of those complaints, 228,400 were likely to be given to legal authorities for criminal investigations. The complaints covered such fraud as credit card and debit card fraud, non-delivery of products or services, and auction fraud.

According to the Internet Crime Complain Center, "The vast majority of cases were fraudulent in nature and involved a financial loss on the part of the complainant. The total dollar loss from all referred cases of fraud was $183.2 million with a median dollar loss of $424.00 per complaint. This is up from $68 million in total reported losses in 2004."

You can learn more about Internet fraud in the United States, and in your state, by visiting the United States Federal Trade Commission at **www. ftc.gov** or by entering the following URL into your search engine (Please note: You will need Adobe Acrobat Reader to read the document.): **www. consumer.gov/idtheft/pdf/CY2005/statemap.pdf**.

There is a legitimate reason for online consumers to worry about Internet fraud. As the owner of a Web-based business, you want to assure your customers that you have taken the necessary steps to protect them against Internet fraud and identity theft. You can do so in a number of ways, including engaging the services of a company that secures an online business's transactions.

ENCRYPTION

Your customers are going to depend on you to ensure their personal information is secure. Another way to make sure your customer's information is safe is to utilize a Web host that promises encryption. Encryption ensures that when you send out an e-mail or other information, the recipient is the only person who will be able to see that information. Thus, private information is protected from hackers and identity thieves.

SHOW YOUR VISITORS YOUR SITE IS SECURE

Your customers want assurance that their personal information, including their credit card information, is going to be safe. A privacy policy is essential to assuaging your customers' peace of mind, but you can also take it a step further and have an outside entity certify that you are actually complying with your privacy policy.

Two of the most popular verification companies are VeriSign and TRUSTe.

VeriSign

Assure your customers that your utmost concern is for the safety of their personal information, which may include their credit card numbers, by teaming with a security company, like VeriSign, and earning certification that lets customers know you protect their personal information.

VeriSign offers dozens of services designed to help Web-based businesses offer their customers' peace of mind when sharing their personal and financial information. Among the many programs are VeriSign's SSL Certificates, designed to offer secure e-commerce for businesses and their customers.

SSL, which stands for Secure Sockets Layer, offers three main things:

1. Encryption. With an SSL Certificate, you and your customers are assured that all personal and sensitive information will be encrypted during online transactions.

2. Your SSL Certificate will provide authenticated and unique information about you, the owner of the certificate.

3. If you purchase an SLL Certificate, you will receive documentation that you are the Certificate Authority, which essentially verifies that you, indeed, are the valid owner of the certificate.

Having an SSL certificate helps assure your customers that all their personal information – credit card numbers, addresses, phone numbers, birthdays, etc. – is safe when they complete an online transaction. Your SSL certificate will be unique from every other business that has an SSL certificate. All SSL certificates are ultimately issued by the Certificate Authority (CA). When you purchase an SSL certificate, you will be given a VeriSign secured seal that you can then display prominently on your Web site.

VeriSign also offers a free trial certificate, valid for up to two weeks, which you can sign up for on their Web site. You can learn more about securing an SSL certificate at VeriSign's Web site: **www.verisign.com**.

VeriSign also offers Identity Protection with "VeriSign Identity Protection." As discussed earlier in the chapter, customers are becoming increasingly concerned about the threat of identity theft and online fraud.

Essentially, "VeriSign Identity Protection," using the latest technology, automatically detects fraudulent transactions and logins while ensuring those customers who are legitimate have an easy, safe online experience.

You can learn more about VeriSign's "Identity Protection" program at their Web site: **www.verisign.com.au/vip/auth.shtml**.

TRUSTe

Another way you can show customers your site is secure is to apply for privacy seals with TRUSTe. With the motto "Make Privacy Your Choice," TRUSTe offers privacy seals to those Web-based and traditional businesses that meet their strict requirements. Once you are given a seal, however, your Web site will continue to be monitored to ensure it remains up to par with TRUSTe's standards.

For example, you may opt to apply for the "Web Privacy Seal." The application process includes three steps:

1. The first step to earning the TRUSTe "Web Privacy Seal" requires you to complete a privacy assessment. Essentially, you will need to give the privacy policy that is posted on your Web site to TRUSTe for review. If you do not yet have a privacy policy, you will need to create one. In addition to your privacy policy, you must also allow your Web site visitors to have a choice by requesting that they consent to how you are going to use their personal information. Finally, you must post a notice disclosing

that you are collecting personal information and how you are going to use that information.

2. You must agree to allow a TRUSTe representative to review your Web site. Following the audit, the representative will contact you and advise you of any changes that you should make before you are issued a "Web Privacy Seal."

3. Once you have had your audit and made the necessary changes, you will be issued a "Web Privacy Seal." However, that is not the end of your relationship with TRUSTe. In fact, your site will be continually monitored to ensure it remains on par with the standards set by TRUSTe.

Another benefit of TRUSTe's "Web Privacy Seal" is the company will act as a mediator in cases of a dispute between you and a customer, offering an alternative to you and the customer going through the court process.

TRUSTe also offers an e-mail privacy seal. Unfortunately, many consumers are wary of sharing their information online because of the fear of getting spammed. If you have an e-mail account, you likely deal with dozens of spam messages a day. In addition to spam being an annoyance, it is also illegal according to the CAN-SPAM Act of 2003. You certainly do not want to become known as the business that spams its customers, whether you decide to apply for the "E-mail Privacy Seal" or not.

To qualify for the "E-mail Privacy Seal," you must agree to several strict requirements, among them:

1. If you send promotional or commercial e-mail, you must have prior approval from the recipients to send such messages.

2. You must have an "Unsubscribe" link that allows recipients to easily and quickly unsubscribe from your e-mail list. You have

ten days from the date of the request to actually remove the recipient from your e-mail list.

3. You must inform your visitors, both in your privacy policy and on the exact page where a request for a visitor's e-mail address is located, if you will be sharing collected e-mail addresses with third parties and the type and nature of e-mails your visitors can expect.

As with the "Web Privacy Seal," you will be required to go through a thorough review process before you are given the "E-mail Privacy Seal." Of course, this is just a brief overview of the "Web Privacy Seal" and "E-mail Privacy Seal" programs. You can learn more about the "E-mail Privacy Seal" and TRUSTe's other programs at **www.truste.org/requirements. php#req5**.

You can learn more about TRUSTe by visiting their Web site at **www. truste.org/businesses/seal_programs_overview.php**.

FIREWALLS: PROTECTING YOUR COMPUTER

Unless your computer is protected by a firewall, you and your information are at risk every time you are connected to the Internet (which is a considerable length of time, if your Internet is connected wirelessly and is always on). In essence, firewalls provide a barrier between your computer and the Internet, and the firewall's main purpose is to protect your computer from viruses, worms, and hackers. Firewalls prevent unwanted information from being downloaded to your hard drive and block the access of undesirable and dangerous Web sites to your computer.

To protect your computer and your Web-based business from unwanted hazards, you must make use of a firewall and ensure it is always up-to-date. Following are some of he most popular firewalls on the market today.

POPULAR FIREWALLS

Microsoft Windows Firewall

Windows Firewall comes on all computers with XP, and it is automatically turned on. However, you can easily turn it off or add a list of exceptions, such as Web sites (America Online, for example) that you do not want the firewall to block.

Essentially, when another person or another computer attempts to connect to your computer, Microsoft Windows Firewall will block what Microsoft calls an unsolicited request. For example, if you use an instant messenger like Skype or ICQ and if you have the firewall turned on, you will be asked by the firewall if you prefer to allow or block the connection.

To learn more about Microsoft Windows Firewall and for a tutorial on how to use it, visit Microsoft at **www.microsoft.com/windowsxp/using/ networking/security/winfirewall.mspx**.

Norton Internet Security Personal Firewall

Norton Internet's Personal Firewall protects your computer from hackers and automatically detects threats such as worms, viruses, and Trojan horses. The personal firewall also eliminates those annoying pop-up and banner ads that often slow down a computer and provides patches for holes in software.

Norton Internet Security Personal Firewall is sold as a subscription, and you have the option of auto renewing your subscription. Norton also offers a free trial of the Norton Personal Firewall 2006, which you can download at **www.symantec.com/home_homeoffice/products/overview.jsp?pcid= is&pvid=npf2006**.

Make sure you check the system requirements to ensure your computer will support the firewall.

Check Point Zone Alarm Internet Security Suite

Check Point Zone Alarm Internet Security Suite's main features include: basic and advanced network and program firewalls, an operating system firewall, anti-virus and anti-spyware protection, protection from identity theft, e-mail security, wireless PC protection, and anti-spam and anti-phishing.

You can purchase a subscription of Check Point Zone Alarm Internet Security Suite at **www.zonelabs.com/store/content/home.jsp**. A one year subscription includes the firewall and a year of updates. You do have to pay extra for each additional computer that will use the firewall. Check Point also offers a free 15-day trial.

McAfee Personal Firewall Plus

McAfee Personal Firewall Plus offers users a wide range of benefits such as: pre-set security levels, automatic updates, identity theft protection, intrusion detection, advanced worm protection, and free instant message tech support. The firewall also monitors all incoming and outgoing communication to protection against hackers, spyware, and viruses.

To purchase an annual subscription to McAfee Personal Firewall plus, visit McAfee's Web site at **www.mcafeestore.com/dr/sat3/ec_MAIN.Entry10 ?V1=761606&PN=1&SP=10023&xid=49745&CUR=702&DSP=&P GRP=0&ABCODE=&CACHE_ID=0**.

9

THE IMPORTANCE OF SEARCH ENGINES

Everyone who uses the Internet uses a search engine. And it is fair to say that everyone with a Web site wants his or her Web site to rank at the top of the search engines. Unfortunately, there is no one set of calculations that search engines — like Google or Yahoo — use to rank Web sites. These calculations are referred to as algorithms. In short, algorithms are confidential calculations that search engines use to determine ranking. The algorithms are kept highly confidential and are changed periodically to ensure that no one abuses the system and so all Web sites have a chance in the rankings.

While no one knows for sure what algorithms determine the rankings, many people believe that ranking high can be attributed to such factors as a Web site's copy and links. Even though you cannot know what specifically you have to do to rank high in the search engines, you can take action to make your Web site more attractive to the search engines, including: submitting keyword rich articles to article directories, using keyword rich content on your Web site, and exchanging links with relevant Web sites.

Keyword Rich Articles

Before you can write keyword rich content, you must know what keywords are: Keywords are specific words or phrases that Internet users use when searching for a Web site specific to their needs. For example, if you are in the market to buy a house, you might go to Google and type in "homes for sale." On the right side of your page will be a list of paid ads that have the words "homes for sale" in their copy. The rest of the page will feature Web sites related to your search.

Keyword rich articles are an excellent way to promote your Web site. After you write an article, you submit it to online article directories. Your article will be accepted and will become a part of the database of free articles that Web masters can then use on their Web sites. The one stipulation is that Web masters must include your author bio box, which will include a link to your Web site, when they post your articles on their Web sites.

When someone types in your keyword or keyword phrase into a search engine, your article (in the database) will appear. The goal is to have the person click on your article, read it, and go to your Web site.

(In Chapter Eleven, "Marketing Your Web-based Business," we will discuss how writing articles can help establish you as an expert in your niche and how to write an effective author bio box.)

Before you write any articles, you must determine what keywords to include in the copy. Remember, keywords are words or phrases your target audience is likely to type into search engines when looking for information on your niche topic.

You can find out what keywords are most popular by utilizing such tools as Word Tracker (**www.wordtracker.com**). Word Tracker requires a paid subscription, but you can go for a trial run to see if it works for you.

Say you are using Word Tracker to determine what keywords are best for your article(s). You may plug in the keyword "dog" and Word Tracker will provide you with a list of all the search keywords that included the word "dog," how many people searched for each keyword or keyword phrase, and exactly how many other Web sites are competing for the same target audience.

The trick is not to use the most popular keywords because you will have much more competition. Rather, choose a keyword or keyword phrase that is popular but does not have as many competitors.

Choose several keywords or keyword phrases you want to use, and you are ready to start writing keyword rich articles. Keyword rich means you use the keywords in your copy several times. For example, make sure your title includes your keywords. You also want to use the keyword at least in the first and final paragraphs. Many, however, try to use the keywords or keyword phrase in every paragraph.

The key to a successful keyword rich article is to focus on the content of the article, which does not have to be longer than 400 or 500 words. Provide your readers with valuable information that they can use so they will want to click on your link in your author bio box and go to your Web site.

Many times people are more focused on how many keywords are in the text rather than the quality of the article. Do not use so many keywords that your article becomes stilted and unreadable.

The Internet is filled with article directories to which you can submit your articles. Here are a few to get you started:

- Ezine Articles – **ezinearticles.com/**

- Go Articles – **www.goarticles.com/**

- Article Dashboard – **www.articledashboard.com/**

- Article Pros – **www.articlepros.com/**

- Article Alley – **www.articlealley.com/**

- Add Articles – **www.add-articles.com/**

Keyword Rich Web Content

Another way to make your Web site attractive to the search engines is to ensure your Web content is also rich with keywords. Again, your content should offer something of value to your visitors, and it must be relevant to your Web site. If your Web site focuses on dogs, write and use keywords about dogs.

Include relevant keywords in your articles. Do not write fluff with keywords thrown in just to get the search engines' attention. It will not work. Such pages are commonly known as "pointer pages," and the search engines frown upon them.

But do not limit your keywords to your Web content. Make sure you include your keywords in your Web site address. For example, if you are selling dog bowls, buy a domain like www.dogbowls.com or www.cheapdogbowls. com. You should also include your keywords in your page title and in your Web site's meta tags.

Link Exchange

One of the ways to potentially rank higher in the search engines is to include links from relevant sites on your Web site. The quantity of links is important, but the quality of the links is probably even more important.

Find Web sites that are relevant to your own Web site. You are looking for quality Web sites with a strong reputation. For example, link to a popular, professional site like **www.cnn.com** rather than your old college roommate's Web site.

Do not link to sites that have little or nothing to do with your Web site. First, they are irrelevant. Second, your ranking in the search engines is likely going to suffer. If you are faced with either having less links that are of a high quality or more links that are of a lower quantity, use less links of a higher quality.

Avoid linking to Web sites that allow anyone to link to them. Many of the links are going to be irrelevant, and linking to such Web sites is only going to pull down your own ranking.

SUBMIT YOUR WEB SITE TO SEARCH ENGINES

The search engines have to know your Web site exists before it can be ranked. Therefore, you must submit your Web site to the search engines or pay to have someone do it for you. Before you begin submitting your Web site address to search engines, however, prepare a brief 25 word description of it that includes your keywords.

You can start by submitting your Web site's URL to the following search engines:

- Google – **www.google.com/addurl/**

- Yahoo – **search.yahoo.com/info/submit.html**

- MSN – **submitit.bcentral.com/msnsubmit.htm**

- Exact Seek – **www.exactseek.com/add.html**

- Alta Vista – **www.altavista.com/addurl/default**

- AlltheWeb – **www.alltheweb.com/help/webmaster/submit_site**

- Open Directory – **dmoz.org/add.html**

- Netscape – **wp.netscape.com/escapes/search/addsite.html**

There are also companies – such as Add Me (**www.addme.com**) and Submit Express (**www.submitexpress.com**) that will submit your Web site to the search engines on a periodic basis, generally for a monthly fee.

KEEP TRACK OF YOUR WEB VISITORS

Keeping track of your Web site visitors is essential. If you do not know how many people are visiting your Web site, you are not going to know if your tactics are working. Some Web hosting packages include statistics counters or the ability to view your traffic.

If your Web host does not offer such an option, you can find software online that will allow you to download a stats counter. There are also stats counters that silently track your visitor count.

To find Web traffic analysis tools for your Web site, you can start by visiting the following sites:

- Stat Counter – **www.statcounter.com**

- Open Tracker – **www.opentracker.net/index.jsp**

- One Stat – **www.onestat.com**

- Add Free Stats – **www.addfreestats.com**

- Benchmark Tracking – **www.benchmarktracking.com**

- ROI Tracking Pro – **www.roi-tracking-pro.com**

Before you choose a stat counters, you may want to do some research to find out what other people are saying about the counter. If the software you are considering requires you to pay, check out the company's reputation on the Better Business Bureau to see if they have a track record and, if so, whether it is good or bad.

PAY-PER-CLICK ADVERTISING

Pay-per-click advertising is a popular way for online businesses to market themselves. It is also a surefire way to get you to the top of the search engines for your particular keywords.

In a nutshell, here is how pay-per-click advertising works:

1. You choose a PPC program. The three most popular are Google, Yahoo Search Marketing, and MSN adCenter.

2. You bid on keywords you think your target market is going to search for when they are looking for products or services similar to yours. For example, if you sell digital cameras, you might choose the keywords "digital camera." You should also consider using commonly misspelled versions of your keywords.

3. You create an ad, using the keywords you have identified as ones your target market will likely use to search.

4. You set a per-click amount. Per-click prices typically start anywhere from one cent to 50 cents per click. Those keywords that are most popular, however, can cost substantially more money.

5. Your ad is displayed as a sponsored ad on the search engine – generally on the right side of the Internet screen or above the normal search results.

6. You pay for every click a visitor makes. If you bid 25 cents per click and 100 people click on your ad, you would pay $25.

7. Monitor the success of your PPC campaign. If you are not getting many clicks, change the keywords or readjust your approach until you find keywords that drive the traffic you want to your Web site.

A word of caution: It is best to set a budget before you even sign up for a pay-per-click advertising program. If you do not have a lot of money at the outset, consider using PPC after you have made some revenue. If you are limited on funds but still want to test PPC, make sure you only pay for what you can afford. Some people get so excited at the concept of advertising their business that they spend far more than they can afford.

Google Adwords

Google Adwords is the most popular pay-per-click advertising program, and it is relatively simple to understand and to implement. If you are going to promote your Web-based business through Google Adwords, you will first need to sign up for an account with the program, which you can do by visiting **adwords.google.com/select/Login**.

Once you have created an account, you will create your ad or ads. To ensure maximum exposure to your ads, you must choose keywords. You can decide which keywords you want to use with the aid of Google's Keyword Tool. With the Keyword Tool, you can type in the keywords you are considering and find out the estimated cost of the keyword and the anticipated position of the ad.

For example, if you are going to use "digital camera" for your keywords, you will be in either the first, second, or third spot on the search results if you pay $0.79 per click. Add an "s" to digital camera, and you will have to pay $0.97 for the same spot. As you can see, your ad is displayed depending on how much you pay per click.

You can set a daily budget with Google Adwords, so you do not have to worry about spending more than you can afford. If you can only afford a few dollars a day, start with that amount. You will also set a budget for each click. For example, if your daily budget is $10, you may want to cap your per click budget at $0.20 per click.

If you only want to target your local market, you can do that or you can target the entire Internet. Google also makes it easy for you to track your results and to edit your keywords and ads as many times as it takes to get the traffic you want.

Yahoo Search Marketing

Yahoo Search Marketing is similar to Google Adwords in the way it works; your ads will be displayed as "Sponsored Results," which are shown on the right side of Yahoo's pages. Like Google Adwords, you can decide whether you want to have your ads target customers in a specific location (i.e. New York City or the east coast) or you want them to target the entire Internet.

Once you make that decision, you will choose your keywords and set your daily budget and your per click budget. You do have some limitations for your ad: a total of 40 characters is permissible for your headline/title and up to 70 characters for your ad's text. Remember, you can tweak your keywords and your ad as needed to get the results that you want.

You can learn more and sign up for Yahoo Search Marketing at: **searchmarketing.yahoo.com**.

Microsoft's adCenter

The latest contender in pay-per-click programs is Microsoft's adCenter, and it works much like Google Adwords and Yahoo Search Marketing. To use Microsoft's PPC, you simply:

1. Choose your keywords and create your ad.

2. Set your daily budget and the price you want to pay each time a customer clicks on your ad.

3. You can target a specific location, a particular age group, gender, or the time and day of the week. However, if you opt to have your ads targeted, you have to pay for it, similar to how you place a bid for the pay-per-click ad itself.

As with Google and Yahoo, you only have to pay when a customer clicks on your ad. You can learn more about Microsoft's adCenter at: **adcenter. microsoft.com/Default.aspx#**.

10

CREATING POWERFUL CONTENT FOR YOUR WEB SITE

People are always in a hurry today — there is never enough time for all the things that have to be done in a day, and the last thing consumers want is to have to tread through Web content that is filled with fluff and takes far too long to get to the point. Faced with treading through fluff or clicking the back button, most consumers are going to do the latter.

Your Web content, particularly your homepage, is likely the first impression a customer is going to get of your business. Ensuring you have clear, concise, and effective Web content is the key to making that first impression a good one.

Tips for Writing Powerful Web Content

Even if you are not a professional writer, you can write powerful Web content if you know what you are doing. First, writing Web content is a whole different ballgame than writing for print, such as a newspaper article or a report. Web readers generally tend to move fast, often scanning content as they try to digest as much information as possible as quickly they can.

When you are writing your Web content, consider your target audience. Is your target audience mostly comprised of women? Men? Teens? Is your target market middle class? Upper middle class? Does your audience tend to have advanced degrees or are they high school graduates? By this point in the process, you should already have a clear understanding of who your target audience is and that is the first step in creating content specifically for your readers.

Keep the following tips in mind when you begin to write your Web content:

1. Prepare an outline before you begin writing. Not all writers like outlines and neither may you. But if you have trouble starting to write, take the time to map out exactly what you want to convey to your audience.

2. Decide how long you want each page to be before you begin to write. Limiting yourself to a certain number of words will help ensure that your copy is tight and without unnecessary fluff.

3. Keep your content concise and your sentences short. Your goal is to get your message across to your audience in as few words as possible. Leave out the flowery language and get to the point. Your readers will be able to recognize fluff when they see it.

4. Do not start every sentence the same way. For example, if you start every sentence with "the," "there," or a noun, you risk losing your audience to boredom. Rather, vary your sentences by also using verbs, adjectives, and adverbs.

5. Talk to your audience in the second person. Instead of saying, "Consumers will enjoy a plethora of benefits from this product," say "You'll enjoy a plethora of benefits when you purchase this product."

6. Write in an inverted pyramid. That means you write all of the essential information in the beginning paragraphs. Journalists who write for newspapers are taught to write in the inverted pyramid because if the editor has to cut the story for length, none of the pertinent information is lost. Write in the inverted pyramid in case your audience does not read the entire page.

7. Write in the active voice. Instead of saying, "An innovative way to keep in touch with clients was designed by my business," say, "My business designed an innovative way to keep in touch with clients."

8. Your content should emphasize the benefits your target market will enjoy when doing business with you.

Once you have written a first draft, put it aside for a day or two. Then come back and look at it with fresh eyes to determine what works and what does not. Identify those areas that could be stronger and revise them. One of the biggest parts of the writing process is rewriting.

When you are confident your copy is strong and powerful, put it aside again for a day or two then proofread it to ensure there are no errors.

The Power of Proofreading

Once you have written your Web copy, take the time to thoroughly proofread it for any grammatical, spelling, or punctuation errors. Remember, however, that proofreading your own work can often be a challenge. Because you know what you have written, you are likely going to miss a typo here or a misspelled word there. One way of catching errors is to read what you have written aloud.

Or consider having someone else proofread your copy before you publish it. Even if you have to hire a freelancer to proofread your content, spend the money. The last thing you want to do is simply publish your Web pages without having them proofread.

You also want to make sure you are using your words the right way. For example:

- It's versus its

- You're versus your

- They're versus their versus there

- Who's versus whose

- Lose versus loose

The importance of proofreading can never be emphasized enough. Think of it this way. If you visited a business's Web site (or any Web site for that matter) that was riddled with errors – spelling mistakes, typos, a lack of punctuation, poor grammar – would you want to do business with that company or individual?

If a Web site owner does not take the time to properly have his Web site proofread, he is not going to give many visitors the confidence they need to do business with him. Everyone makes mistakes, but there is absolutely no excuse for an error-ridden Web site.

If you are not a writer but want to write your own Web content, you may want to purchase one of the most revered books in the writing industry: *The Elements of Style* by William Strunk, E.B. White, and Roger Angell.

SHOULD YOU HIRE SOMEONE ELSE TO WRITE YOUR WEB CONTENT?

Because your Web content is a powerful tool, you want to make sure it is as professional as possible. That means if you are not confident that you have the skills to write compelling content, you may want to consider hiring a professional writer.

Hiring a Professional Writer

Hiring a professional writer is a big decision, but it certainly does not have to be a stressful experience. The first thing you want to do is find out what you need a professional writer for: Write a project description, detailing exactly what you need from the writer, a tentative deadline for the first draft, and a tentative deadline for the final draft.

A project description will help you and the writer. It will give you clarity as to what you need and will make it easier for the writer to give you an accurate price estimate. Just as important, it will ensure the writer you hire has a clear idea of what you expect from him or her.

When choosing a writer, take the following factors into consideration:

- **Experience.** How much and what type of experience does the writer have? You do not necessarily want to count out new writers, but you should find out what type of experience each writer possesses. A writer may not have a lot of experience, but his or her enthusiasm and writing samples may make up for it.

- **Expertise.** Is the writer familiar with your niche? Expertise is not always necessary for a writer to write powerful content, but in some cases – such as with technical, medical, or legal copy – you will certainly need someone with expertise. If you cannot find a writer with expertise in your niche, consider someone who is knowledgeable in a similar area.

- **Portfolio.** Ask potential candidates for a portfolio of writing samples. Most writers have their own styles, and you will likely find a writer with a style you prefer. (Just a note: By considering new writers, you may find a writer who has the talent and the knowledge you are looking for but does not have the experience. Writing samples can be just as important, if not more important, than experience.)

- **Price.** A professional writer is not cheap. Keep in mind that the writer with the cheapest fee is not necessarily going to give you the highest quality. Unless you are extremely strapped for money, you should not base your decision solely on price.

Keep in mind that you might not find the perfect writer for your needs, but you will likely find a writer who is a good fit for your needs.

You can generally find professional writers through your local Chamber of Commerce; by asking friends, family, or coworkers for recommendations; by flipping through your local yellow pages; by searching for "professional writers" online; or by using one of the popular online bidding sites we listed earlier.

11

MARKETING YOUR WEB-BASED BUSINESS

O nce you have published your Web site and have officially declared your Web-based business open, you are going to have to work hard to build a loyal customer base. There are dozens of marketing methods — both free and those requiring funds — you can use to get the word out about your Web-based business.

Do not limit yourself to one marketing strategy. Try several strategies at the same time and evaluate them to see which is working best for you. There are many marketing strategies that are easy to implement and that will get your Web-based business the publicity it needs to build a loyal customer base.

Following are some of the best ways to publicize your Web-based business. Remember, however, that marketing is an ongoing process, and it is going to play a role as long as you are in business. Once you create a loyal customer base, you must continue to market to retain your current customers and to gain new ones.

CREATE A LOGO

Creating a logo is something you can and should do before you even open your virtual doors, and it is a great tool for creating brand recognition.

Unfortunately, many new business owners decide to wait to have their logo created until they have developed a small customer base.

Stop and think about several popular logos for a second. McDonald's has golden arches. Macintosh has an apple. Pillsbury has the Doughboy. Coke has the bottle. Nike has a swoosh. The list goes on. The point is people remember those logos. The cited logos are all simple graphics, but they are powerful and effective.

Benefits of a Logo

Instead of waiting until you have the money or until your business grows, create a logo now. You want to create a business logo because:

1. Your logo will create brand recognition, making it much easier for potential customers to remember who you are. You will be able to display your logo on your Web site and on all your marketing materials, including letterhead, brochures, business cards, etc.

2. A logo is going to help you stand out among your competition, especially if your competition does not have a logo.

3. If your business is small, a logo is going to make it appear larger.

4. If it is difficult to discern your business purpose from your business name, your logo can help show what your business offers.

5. When you have a logo, you will appear more established to potential customers.

Logo Design

Even if you do not have a large budget, you may still be able to afford a professionally designed logo. You may be able to find a professional graphic designer who will be willing to work within your budget at one of several bidding sites.

However, if you cannot afford to pay for a logo at the onset, there are ways you can easily and affordably design your own logo. If you are going to design a logo yourself, you will need to take several factors into consideration during the design process:

- Does your logo or idea clearly and effectively convey your company's image?

- Will your logo look just as good in black and white as it does in color?

- Do you have the ability to make your logo larger or smaller, depending on your needs, without losing its quality? For example, will your logo look just as good on a pen as it does on a calendar?

- Is your logo visually appealing? Will it interest your customers and make them look at your logo again?

- Does the logo look as good on the printed page (i.e. brochures, letterhead, business cards) as it does online (i.e. Web site, blog)?

Remember, you do not need an intricate logo. Simple is best. Before you officially launch your logo, get feedback from family, friends, and others who will be honest.

Logo Design Resources

- Logo Design Studio – **www.snapfiles.com/get/logodesignstudio. html**

- Logo Creator – **www.thelogocreator.com**

- Corporate Identity Creator – **www.cicreator.com**

- AAA Logo – Logo Design Software – **www.aaa-logo.com**

- Mix FX – Flash Logo Design – **www.mix-fx.com/flash-logos-design/flashlogos.html**

WRITE ARTICLES AND SUBMIT TO ARTICLE DIRECTORIES

Another easy and free, albeit time consuming, way to promote your Web-based business is to create articles and submit them to e-zines and article directories. (Read the chapter on "Search Engines" for tips on how to write keyword rich articles.) The benefits of writing articles and submitting them are varied. First, you will have the opportunity to further establish yourself as an expert in your niche. Experts are often revered and trusted sources of information, another huge benefit.

Some article directories will allow you to use embedded links or hyperlinks in the article's text. A hyperlink is a link that points to a specific Web site or to another part of the same Web site. (Hyperlinks, however, are not limited to the Internet; you can also use hyperlinks within Word and other offline documents.)

To create a hyperlink, highlight the word or words that you want users to click to take them to a specific Web site. After highlighting the word or words, right click with your mouse and click on "Hyperlink." A page called "Insert Hyperlink" will open, and you will simply type the Web site address to which you want to link. When the hyperlink is displayed, it will usually turn blue and become underlined.

You can make use of hyperlinks in articles you submit to directories that allow the embedded links in the articles themselves. For example, if you sell editing services with your Web-based business, you might decide to write an article on the benefits of hiring an editor. When you use the word "editor" in your article, you might want to hyperlink it to your Web site.

By submitting articles you are also getting free publicity. When you submit an article to an article directory, you can include your business information in the author bio box. The author bio box is especially important if you are not allowed to use embedded links in your articles.

Your author bio box is an opportunity for you to succinctly tell readers why they should visit your Web site, and it should include:

- Your name.

- Your Web site address.

- Your Unique Selling Proposition (USP). For example, Domino's Pizza's USP used to be "Your pizza delivered in 30 minutes or it's free."

- A call to action. For example, "Visit my Web site now where you can download a free report on the benefits of hiring a professional editor."

Create an author bio box that is as specific and as concise as possible. A good author bio box will help drive traffic to your Web site.

PURCHASE OR CREATE BUSINESS CARDS

Your business may be Web-based, but that does not mean you should forget about marketing in the offline world. Business cards are essential for any businessperson — online and offline. The good news is purchasing a professional business card is not expensive.

A quick search online will lead you to dozens of companies that offer quality business card printing at inexpensive prices. If you would rather create your own business card, you can do so easily if you have a quality printer and stock paper.

Once you have your business cards, use them. The rule of thumb is to give two business cards to everyone you meet: One for the person you are giving the business cards to and another business card for that person to give to someone else.

There are two main opinions as to how to best utilize the space on a business card. One side believes that both sides of the business card should be used. Others believe it is best to leave the backside of a business card blank to allow people to jot down notes, such as where they met you and when.

Regardless of whether you use one side or both sides, make use of business cards. Carry them wherever you go. You never know when you might meet a potential client.

JOIN YOUR LOCAL CHAMBER OF COMMERCE

Most cities and towns have local chapters of the Chamber of Commerce. There is also the U.S. Chamber of Commerce, an organization that accredits local chapters and associations. The national and local chapters of the Chamber of Commerce are dedicated to helping businesses.

Joining a local chapter of the Chamber of Commerce will give you numerous opportunities to network with other members (who may turn out to be potential clients) through member events. For example, some chapters of the Chamber of Commerce hold monthly gatherings, with the meeting being held at a different member's business each month.

Local chapters of the Chamber of Commerce also offer numerous benefits for members, including discounted advertising opportunities, the chance to have their businesses in the Chamber's member directory, access to affordable health insurance, and other programs beneficial to business owners.

You can find the U.S. Chamber of Commerce online at **www.uschamber. com**. Joining the national Chamber of Commerce affords discounts on various products (a discount on FedEx shipping, for example), offers affordable healthcare options, and keeps members apprised of the latest news that affects your business.

You can do a search for your local Chamber of Commerce by visiting the national Chamber of Commerce or you can simply type "(your town) Chamber of Commerce" into any search engine.

NETWORK

Networking is an essential part of business. When you network, you cultivate business relationships with other business owners and build your credibility. Your business relationship should benefit you and the other business owner. For example, say you attend a networking event held by your local Chamber of Commerce. You mingle and meet a cartoonist who is working on a children's book. The only problem is, he admits, he cannot write very well. You tell him you are a writer. By the end of the event, you have exchanged numbers to further discuss teaming up to work on the children's book together. That is networking, and it is extremely effective.

Networking Ideas

As we just discussed, an effective way to network is to join your local Chamber of Commerce and attend networking events. But there are numerous other ways you can network — both online and offline:

- Always carry your business cards with you.

- Use your business cards. Always give two business cards to the other person — one for him or her and another for him to pass along.

- You can literally network anywhere. For example, you might be waiting for your plane to board at the airport, and you strike up a conversation with a fellow passenger. Perhaps he is in your industry or knows someone who is.

- Ask for referrals. When someone gives you a referral, make note of who that person is and contact the referral as soon as possible. But do not just ask for referrals; you also want to give referrals. Remember, networking should benefit the other person as well.

- Attend industry conferences and trade shows.

- Write articles to establish yourself as an expert in your niche. Identify local publications — such as newspapers and magazines — whose readers could benefit from your particular expertise, then write an article and submit it to those publications. Your first article may be rejected. You might be rejected several times, but keep trying. Once you get published, promote that fact.

- Blog.

- Join and participate in clubs and organizations in your industry.

- Volunteer in local organizations to increase your visibility in the community.

- Join and participate in online forums related to your niche.

This is by no means a comprehensive list of ways you can network. You will likely discover other networking opportunities in your own community and online as you market your Web-based business.

Tips for Successful Networking

Networking is more than just meeting people and passing around business cards. There is a distinct difference between someone who is successful at networking and someone who has poor results with networking. For success with networking, keep these tips in mind:

- Follow up on your referrals.

- Be positive. You will attract far more people if you are positive than if you are negative.

- Just be yourself. Do not put on airs and try to be something you are not.

- Effectively communicate. Talk and listen to those with whom you are networking.

- Always be on the look out for networking opportunities — whether you are at the dog park with your dog, at a sporting event, or at the grocery store.

- Show your customers you appreciate their business. Customers who feel you value their business are more likely to refer you to others.

- Keep in touch with those you have met through networking. Drop them an e-mail or give them a call to find out how they are doing and let them know what is new with your business.

- Be sincere when you are talking to others and show a genuine interest in what they have to offer.

- When you are given a business card, flip it over and jot down some information about the person who has given it to you: where you met him or her, brief details about what he or she does, etc.

Successful networking also requires persistence, and it is hard work. Do not give up if you do not succeed at your first networking event. The more you network, the better and the more successful you will become.

Networking Resources

There are plenty of networking resources available to you — from your local Chamber of Commerce to online organizations that offer opportunities for business owners to meet and network.

- Ryze Business Networking – **www.ryze.com**

- BNI International (The Business Referral Organization) – **www.bni.com/**

- Toastmasters (ideal if you have trouble with public speaking) –**www.toastmasters.org**

- LeTip International – **www.letip.com/**

- The U.S. Chamber of Commerce – **www.uschamber.com**

- The Minority Business Network – **www.mbnet.com**

- The Entrepreneurs' Organization – **www.eonetwork.org**

- International Federation of Small & Medium Enterprises – **www.ifosme.org**

- Peer Sight – **www.peersightonline.com**

- The Small Business Community Forums – **www. smallbusinessforums.org**

JOIN THE BETTER BUSINESS BUREAU (ONLINE)

The Better Business Bureau is a leading source for customers who want to find information on the companies with which they are considering doing business. Customers are allowed to file complaints with the Better Business Bureau, citing their grievances with a particular business, which means if your customer is checking out your business, he or she will know whether there have been complaints against you.

People trust the Better Business Bureau. It is as simple as that. When businesses are listed with the Better Business Bureau, consumers know that they will have a voice and support should there be a problem with a company that does not respond quickly or effectively.

There are two versions of the Better Business Bureau: the local BBBs and the online Better Business Bureau. To qualify for admission to the online BBB program, you must be a member of your local Better Business Bureau (**www.bbb.org**).

Benefits of Being a Member

The good news is if you are not yet a member of your local BBB, you can apply for admission during the time you apply for the online program. The BBB Online offers businesses several advantages, including:

- Your customers will know that your business is trustworthy.

- Your customers will feel more secure in purchasing from

you because you took the time and effort to become a BBB member.

- Potential customers will easily be able to find you because your business will be listed in the Better Business Bureau Online's directory.

Requirements

To become a member of the BBB Online, you will have to meet numerous requirements, such as being a member of the Better Business Bureau, having been in business for at least a year, and having responded appropriately to any and all customer complaints. You will also have to respond to all complaints in a timely member and agree to dispute resolution.

When you apply for the BBB Online, you must meet all requirements, and you will be required to pay a license fee. The fee will depend on the size of your business. When you are accepted into the BBB Online, you will receive a Reliability Seal that you can then place on your Web site.

You can learn more about the BBB Online and apply for the Reliability Seal at their Web site: **www.bbbonline.org**.

PRESS RELEASES

Press releases are an excellent means of getting the word out about your Web-based business. Writing a strong press release that will get you noticed, rather than a typical press release that will be tossed in the garbage, is something of an art — you must know what editors are looking for in press releases. A good press release can garner you the publicity you need to propel your Web-based business to the next level of success.

Press Release Basics

Your press release should be broken down into four parts: headline, lead paragraph, body, and closing paragraph. Journalists write an inverted pyramid format, and that is exactly what you should do with your press release. Write all the pertinent information in the early paragraphs. That way, if the editor has to cut off some of the press release, the important information is still communicated to your audience.

Let us look at which each part should entail to increase your chances of having an editor read your press release:

- **Headline.** A headline must accomplish several things at one time: It must succinctly summarize your press release, in no more than ten words, in a way that grabs editors' attention and draws them in, compelling them to read further.

- **Lead paragraph.** The lead paragraph is your opportunity to hook the editor and compel him to read further. Your lead paragraph must answer: Who? What? Where? When? Why? How?

- **Body of the press release.** In the body of the press release, you will go into further detail. Remember, make sure you write in the inverted pyramid format, so nothing important is lost if the editor has to cut the press release.

- **Closing paragraph.** Your closing paragraph is your opportunity to succinctly summarize your press release and to include the contact information for your contact person, including name, phone number, e-mail address, and Web site address.

Press Release Writing Tips

If you have never written a press release before, take some time to read other business's press releases. You can find press releases at the links listed in the next section. Once you have an idea of how press releases work, you are ready to start planning/writing your press release. You also want to keep in mind the following when writing your press release:

- Identify the story you want to share in the press release.

- Ask yourself: Is the story newsworthy?

- Will your readers be able to relate to the information you are sharing?

- Write in the third person.

- Steer clear of flowery language. Your press release should be written in short, clear sentences without a lot of adjectives or fluff.

- Stick to the facts. Unnecessary information will only increase your chances of having the press release tossed.

- Use quotes relevant to the story.

- Never make statements that can be misconstrued as advertisements; i.e. "We produce the world's best" anything.

- Make it easy for the media to contact you by providing as many contact details as possible. Ensure your contact information is correct, and there are no typos.

- Be available to talk to the media if you are contacted. Do not send out a press release then go on vacation.

- Edit your press release for content and clarity.

- Proofread to ensure there are no grammar, spelling, or punctuation errors.

Press Release Distribution

In addition to sending your press releases to local media, you should consider submitting them to various online press release sites. The good news is you can submit press releases at some sites for free or for a small fee, while others have a hefty price tag.

Some Web sites simply post the press releases on their site after they have been approved, while others submit them to a search engine. Read the TOS (Terms of Service) before submitting your press release, so you know exactly what you are getting.

Following is just a partial list of press release distribution sites, both free and fee-based, to get you started:

- 24-7 Press Release — **www.24-7pressrelease.com/**

- PR Newswire — **www.prnewswire.com/**

- PR.com — **www.pr.com/press-releases**

- Market Wire — **www.marketwire.com/**

- I-Newswire — **www.i-newswire.com/**

- Business Wire — **home.businesswire.com/portal/site/home/index.jsp?front_door=true**

- PR Web Direct — **www.prwebdirect.com/**

- E-mail Wire — **www.emailwire.com/cgi-bin/news/db.cgi?db=customer**

ONLINE FORUMS AND MESSAGE BOARDS

Message boards (also known as online forums and discussion groups) are another easy, effective, and free way to market your online business. Find message boards and forums that relate to your niche and your target market and sign up for them.

If you have never posted on a message board, you must be aware that there are some basic rules of etiquette that you should follow:

1. Carefully read the message boards TOS (Terms of Service), so you know exactly what you are allowed and not allowed to do. For example, many message boards forbid foul language, spam, pornography, and blatant promotion of one's products or services.

2. Rather than just jumping in and posting on your first visit to the message board, take the time to read and get to know the message board. Keep reading until you have an idea of what posters like to talk about, what they shy away from, who the most popular and respected posters are, and the board's personality. Once you have a feel for the message board, start posting.

3. Do not overtly market your product or service by posting sales-y messages, and do not make your first post about your product or service. Most people in message boards do not like or approve of posters (especially new posters) who blatantly promote their products or services.

4. Make your posts valuable. Do not try to increase your post count by simply posting worthless posts with only a smiley face or to say something like "I agree." Tell the poster *why* you agree. When you take the time to make thoughtful, helpful posts, you are establishing yourself as a valuable member of the online community and as an expert in your niche.

5. If signature files are permitted, create a signature file and use it.

6. Visit the message boards frequently to reply to messages, both those directed at you and at others.

7. When you post, never use ALL CAPS. All caps is akin to shouting. You will only annoy other posters who will likely just ignore your post. It is also very difficult on some people's eyes to read all caps.

8. If you are replying to someone's post, use the button that allows you to quote the post to which you are replying. You may want to snip the post, if it is long, to focus only on the section to which you are replying.

9. Never post your personal information, even in your signature line, such as your full name, your phone number, and your mailing address.

10. Ignore trolls. There are people, commonly referred to as trolls, who frequent message boards merely to annoy other posters. Trolls post rude comments designed to bait you into replying. Just ignore these posters.

You can find message boards by typing "(your niche) message board" into any search engine. Posting to message boards is time consuming, but it is an effective way to establish yourself as an expert in your niche.

YOUR SIGNATURE LINE

Your signature line — whether used at the end of your e-mails or formatted to be included in every post you make on message boards — allows you to give your e-mail recipients important information quickly. A typical e-mail signature line looks something like this:

Your Name

Your Business Name
http://www.website.com

This is my business slogan

Any additional information you want to add (but be brief)

Notice that there are no fancy fonts, no colors, and no photographs or graphics, and that is the way it should be. Keep your signature file brief and basic. There is no need for fluff, as your goal is to indirectly promote your business and your Web site. Additionally, different font sizes, colors, and photos may appear differently, in a bad way, depending on the e-mail program.

When deciding how to create your signature line, keep the following in mind:

- To reiterate, keep your signature line brief. Unless it is absolutely necessary, do not include your phone number, fax number, or cell phone number.

- Avoid anything in your signature line that sounds like a sales pitch. If you want to describe your business or the product or service you offer, do so in a way that will encourage people to visit your Web site.

- Type your name as you would in any professional communication. For example, Jane Doe, not jane doe. You want to convey a professional image, so you must adhere to the correct grammar.

- Your signature file does not need your e-mail address, unless you want people to e-mail you at a different e-mail address.

- When you type in your Web site address, make sure you include the http:// in front of the actual address to ensure that all of your recipients can view it simply by clicking on the link. (Some e-mail programs will not allow you to automatically click a link unless it has the http://.)

Before you use your signature line, proofread it. The last thing you want is to have any errors — spelling, typos, or otherwise — because that just makes you look unprofessional.

Many e-mail programs allow you to save your signature file so it appears every time you send an e-mail. You may want to consider having several signature files. For example, you might have a signature file that you use when you send professional e-mail and another signature file for when you send e-mails to people with whom you have more of a casual relationship.

Take the time to create a signature line now — it is a fast, easy, and free way to market your Web-based business.

BANNER ADVERTISING

Banner ads are rectangular advertisements that are generally placed at the top of a Web page. Banner ads are a popular way of advertising on the Internet. In some instances, you will have to pay for placing banner ads, but if you start an affiliate program, you will have others place them for you in exchange for a commission of the products/services they sell.

Banner ads are purchased in terms of CPM, or Cost Per Thousand Impressions. Essentially, you pay one price for every 1,000 times your ad is viewed, which is also known as impressions.

Banner Ad Creation Tips

To ensure your banner drive traffic to your site and convince consumers to purchase your products or services, make sure your banner ad catches your audience's attention

Less really is more when it comes to banner advertising. Limit the wording on your ad to seven words, and make those words powerful. For example, use words such as incredible, successful, unbelievable, amazing, trusted, or superior. Such words can instill confidence and curiosity in your audience.

Banner ads often include images, but the key to effective images is to have just enough — not too many and not too few. Using too many images will not only make your banner ad look cluttered, but it will take your ad even longer to load on a Web page, something you want to avoid.

You also want to stick with one font or two at the very most, and do not go overboard by using a lot of different colors. You do not want your banner ad to look cluttered.

Placing Your Banner Ads

Once you have created your banner ad, you will need to find Web sites on which to place it. The easiest way to get your banner ads on the Internet is to start an affiliate program. (Chapter Twelve, "Keeping Your Customers Coming Back Again and Again," details how to start an affiliate program.) In a nutshell, your affiliates will promote your products or services for you. One way they can do this is by placing banner ads, that you provide, on their Web sites. If you offer banner ads to your affiliates, make sure you offer the ad in several sizes.

Another way to place your banner ads is to contact Web site owners with an audience similar to your own. While it will take you considerable time and effort, you will be able to control where your banner ads are placed.

You may also want to consider joining a banner ad network. Essentially, banner ad networks work as the go-between between advertisers and Web site owners. The banner ad network places the advertisers' ads on Web sites. The only problem with this approach is you, as the advertiser, will have absolutely no control over where your banner ads are placed. Still, if you do not have the time to place your banner ads on a lot of Web sites, you may want to consider trying a banner ad network, which will cost you some money.

Finally, you can use the services of an advertising agency to promote your ad for you if you have a substantial budget. If you decide to go with an advertising agency, make sure you get information — such as the services the ad agency offers, rates, and overall experience of the agency's employees — from several agencies before choosing the one that best meets your needs.

ONLINE DIRECTORIES

An online directory is the Web equivalent of your local yellow and white pages. Submit your contact and business information to online directories to ensure people who need your products or services can find you. It is free to submit your information to many of the online directories.

You can do an Internet search for "online directories" or start by going to the following Web sites:

- Online Yellow Pages — **www.yp.com**

- Superpages: Yellow Pages & White Pages — **www.superpages. com**

- Jayde.com — **www.jayde.com**

- Where2Go — **www.where2go.com**

- Home Business Directory — **www.links4rank.com**

- Business Week Business Directory — **businessweek.directorym. com**

- Biz Journals Directory — **www.bizjournalsdirectory. com/?source=96**

BLOG

Blogging is one of the most popular Internet activities today — for individuals who want to get their opinions heard and businesses that want to publicize their products or services. Because blogging is a quick and effective way to reach audiences, many businesses have begun to realize that having a blog is essential to staying ahead of the competition.

Essentially, a blog is an online journal in which bloggers discuss whatever is on their mind. For business owners, blogs are a popular way of generating buzz about a product or service and establishing expertise in their particular industry or niche. Blogs are updated frequently. If you choose to have a blog, you can publish new content daily, several times a week, or weekly. It all depends on how much time you have to devote to your blogs.

Benefits of Blogging

Why blog? Ask any business owner or individual who blogs, and you are likely to get a variety of different reasons. As a Web-based business owner, you will find that blogging provides you with such benefits as:

- Feedback. If a reader does not like your latest product idea or thinks your product or service is one of the best in the industry, he can say so easily and quickly by adding a comment that will then be displayed at the end of your blog entry. Other readers will be able to read the comments. Whether positive or negative, feedback can be a valuable tool in determining what your target market wants.

- Fresh content keeps your business in the forefront of your customers' minds.

- With a quality blog, you can effectively build brand recognition.

- You can communicate directly to your target market and build a reputation as an expert in your niche.

- Running a blog is relatively low cost. If you write the entries yourself and publish using free blogging software, you will have no out-of-pocket costs except your time.

- Blogging is a fast way to reach your customers right now.

- You will be able to develop a relationship with your customers. When someone comments on your blog, respond. Open dialogue is critical.

As you begin blogging, you will likely add to the list of benefits. Ultimately, a blog is an inexpensive, effective, and popular marketing tool that will cost you little more than your time.

Business Blogging Tips

Blogging, at least for businesses, is more than just sitting down and writing your thoughts. If you really want to drive traffic to your blog, you must know what an effective, popular blog entails:

- Know your audience. Your target market and those in your niche are your audience.

- Write blog entries that will bring value to your target market; valuable content will help ensure readers visit your blog again and again.

- Discuss current events within your industry.

- Read other industry blogs and post blog entries in response to them. Make sure you provide a link to the blog to which you are referring.

- Show your personality. Instead of writing stiff blogs that read more like a newspaper article, infuse your personality into your blog entries.

- Keywords are essential to getting noticed by the search engines. However, do not use so many keywords that your blog entries appear stilted or does not make sense.

- Build links. Find other quality blogs in your niche or industry, and link to them.

- Update your blog frequently. Your readers want fresh content, so give it to them.

To get an idea for what other businesses in your niche are blogging about, check out other blogs in your industry. You can adapt and change your blog as it grows and you become more familiar with what your target market wants.

Blogging Software

When you purchase Web hosting, find out if it comes with a blog creation tool. Creating a blog from your control panel is as simple as typing the blog name and hitting the "create" or "install" button.

If you do not have Web hosting that allows blog creation or if you would rather go a different route, you can sign up for a free blog. There is a wide variety of free blogging software available. Following are a list of some of the most popular.

In many instances, free blogging software allows you to customize your blog. For example, Word Press offers dozens of templates you can use.

Blogging Resources

- Blogger — **www.blogger.com**

- Word Press — **www.wordpress.com**

- Live Journal — **www.livejournal.com**

- Blog Jet — **www.blogjet.com**

- Blog.com — **www.blog.com**

- Blog-City — **www.blog-city.com**

- Blogster — **www.blogster.com**

Post on Other Blogs

But writing your own blog is not the only way to drive traffic to your Web site. Find other bloggers in your niche, who are not your direct competition, and read their posts. When you reply to a post, also include your name and Web site address. When other people read your comments, they will easily be able to click on your Web site URL and find out about your products or services.

Posting comments does not have to consume a lot of your time, but again, it is an easy, effective, and free means of marketing your Web-based business.

PODCAST

The latest in a long line of technological advances that can benefit your marketing strategy, podcasts are proving to be an effective way of reaching millions of potential customers around the world. In fact, many well-known business entities — including the British Broadcasting Corporation (BBC) and Apple's iTunes — are taking advantage of the ease with which they can reach customers by producing podcasts.

Perhaps even better than the ease with which businesses can reach customers is the fact that customers can download free software with which to listen to the podcasts, making podcasts easily accessible to millions.

Podcasts are audio files, which you can place on your Web site or elsewhere on the Internet, that can be downloaded onto an MP3 player, iPod, or a computer's hard drive. That means your customers and potential customers can download your podcast and listen to it anytime they want.

You can use podcasts just as you use newsletters: as a way to offer customers who opt-in valuable information, related to your niche, that they can use. When a customer subscribes to your podcast, he will be automatically sent the podcast via RSS feeds.

Recording a Podcast

Recording a podcast is actually very easy. All you need is an MP3 player, a headset with a microphone, and a goal. After you have installed your MP3 player on your computer, you plug your headset in and get ready to record.

You will likely want to create a script for your podcasts. Write a script, or have a professional writer do so for you, then practice a few times to familiarize yourself with the text.

Start recording when you are ready, and save it as an MP3 file when you are finished. When you are happy with the podcast, you can upload it to your Web site. And, when you use podcasting software, it will automatically send the podcast to all your subscribers every time you post a new one.

Podcasting Software

You can find podcasting software by visiting:

- BlogMatrix Sparks — **www.blogmatrix.com**

- ePodcast Creator — **www.industrialaudiosoftware.com/ products/epodcastcreator.html**

- RecorderPro — **www.soniclear.com/ProductsRecorderPro. html**

- Record For All — **www.recordforall.com**

- CastBlaster — **www.castblaster.com**

- Audacity — **audacity.sourceforge.net/download**

To find more podcasting software, simply do an online search.

Your subscribers will automatically be informed when you have updated your blog, podcast, or newsletter if you offer them the option of subscribing to RSS feeds.

OFFER REFERRAL INCENTIVES

One of the best, and free, marketing methods is word-of-mouth. You provide a customer with an excellent product or service combined with topnotch customer service, and that customer is likely to tell his or her friends and family about your business.

You can also actively encourage your customers to refer others to your business by offering referral incentives, such as a discount off his or her next purchase. Other incentive ideas include:

- Gift certificates

- Free consultation, if offering a service

- Discounts on your product or service

- Coupons

- A product related to your niche

Brainstorm and use your imagination, and you will likely be able to devise dozens of fun, creative incentives that will encourage your customers to refer others to you. You might also offer an incentive for the customer that has been referred, as well to further encourage him or her to purchase your product or service.

RADIO ADS

If you have the funds, you may want to consider having a radio ad produced and buying airtime. There are numerous advantages to using radio as a means of advertising your Web-based business. Radio advertising is far less expensive than television advertising. It is also extremely easy to make changes to your radio commercial at the last minute, if need be.

When you buy airtime, you are essentially purchasing the time that your commercial is going to be aired. To determine the best time of the day to have your ad aired, find out the demographics and ratings of the specific radio stations you are considering. You can do this by contacting the advertising sales representatives at local radio stations. Avoid telling the sales rep your target market until he or she reveals the station's demographics. If a radio station meets your target market, request a media kit.

While there are distinct advantages to producing and airing a radio commercial, there are some disadvantages. Many people do not listen closely to the radio, especially those who use it for background noise, so you will have to ensure you have a creative jingle or some other way to grab and keep their attention. You also have very limited time to get your message across.

Once you decide that you want to run a radio ad, you will need to write a script, find voice talent, and purchase airtime. Your biggest consideration as to when to purchase airtime is likely going to be the cost. The most expensive times for airing an advertisement are during the morning commute from 5 a.m. to 10 a.m. and the evening commute from 3 p.m. to 7 p.m. In many cases, you will receive a discount if you purchase airtime in blocks or sign an annual contract.

If you cannot afford to run your ad on more than one radio station, do not worry. The key is to run the radio ad consistently throughout a period of several months or more. Airing an ad for only a few weeks then simply pulling it is not going to help you grow your business. Rather, airing your ad over a period of months will help listeners get to know your business, especially if you have a memorable jingle or something that makes your commercial stand out from the competition.

TV COMMERCIALS

You may balk at the thought of producing and running a television advertisement. After all, it is no big secret that TV ads can be hugely expensive. Advertising on network television, while expensive during certain events like the Super Bowl, can actually be quite affordable at times. In fact, for a ten to 60 second television commercial, you can expect to pay anywhere from $90 to $2,500. You will obviously pay more for airtime during the primetime hours, but you will also likely reach a larger audience. If you want to advertise during a primetime drama or sitcom, consider waiting until the shows are in reruns and ask the sales representative for a discount because your commercial will be run during a repeat.

There are distinct advantages to television advertising: You will reach a potentially huge audience; you can be as creative as you want with the ad; and you will be able to brand your business and your product quickly and effectively.

On the downside, you will need to spend a considerable amount of money to produce a professional television ad that airs on network television. Additionally, once your ad is produced, you will find that making any changes can be very expensive.

If you have a substantial budget for advertising, advertising on network TV is an excellent means of reaching your target audience. However, if you cannot yet afford an ad on network television, consider the less expensive alternative: Advertise on cable television where ads can run anywhere from as little as $8 to $2,000.

In most cases, you can purchase ad space from the cable television station or from the program. It all depends on the cable company with which you will be advertising. Contact your local cable companies for more information on their advertising rates.

Finally, if you have a product or service that lends itself to more airtime, you may want to consider producing an infomercial.

NEWSPAPER ADS

Newspaper advertising is another effective way to reach your target audience, and it is still one of the most popular ways for businesses to advertise their products and services. You can expect to pay anywhere from $200 to $20,000, depending on whether you are advertising in a local or national newspaper, how long your ad is slated to run, and other related factors.

Newspaper advertising has a plethora of benefits, including: Ads are often very inexpensive to produce; you can make changes to the ad with relative ease; and newspapers generally offer various ad rates, depending on the ad's size. Advertising in a newspaper allows you to offer your customers coupons, an added incentive for them to visit your Web site.

But you should also be aware of the disadvantages to newspaper advertising. First, you are going to be limited as to what your ad contains mainly because photographs, in particular, do not print always print well on newsprint. (Pick up an edition of your local newspaper to get an idea of the quality of the photographs in advertisements.)

In all likelihood, your ads are going to run alongside your competition's ads, and you may not reach a large readership depending on the day and edition in which your ad runs.

Even if you cannot afford to advertise in a national newspaper or your local daily newspaper, you may want to consider starting by advertising in your local weekly newspaper.

12

KEEPING YOUR CUSTOMERS COMING BACK AGAIN AND AGAIN

The key to any successful Web-based business is building customer loyalty to ensure they return to your business again and again. Even when your customers are not buying from you, you want your business to remain at the forefront of their minds.

There is a plethora of ways to keep your customers returning to you again and again, and many of them are actually free. All they require is effort, some imagination, and time on your part.

SET UP YOUR OWN AFFILIATE PROGRAM

Affiliate programs are an excellent way of getting other people to promote your products or services. You provide each affiliate with banners or links they can place on their Web site to promote your products or services. In exchange for their efforts in promoting your products or services, you offer them a percentage of every sale they make.

Benefits of Affiliate Programs

There are various other benefits to having an affiliate program for your products or services, including:

- With links to your product or service, you will receive a lot of exposure and potentially reach millions of Internet users.

- While your affiliates are busy promoting your products or services, your time is freed to concentrate on other marketing efforts.

- Chances are your sales are going to rise much faster than if you alone were promoting your products or services.

- You do not have to pay anything upfront. Unlike traditional advertising where you have to pay upfront, you do not pay your affiliates until after they have made the sales.

- The opportunity for unlimited growth exists. If your affiliate program is of high quality, you will attract more and more affiliates who may refer other affiliates to you.

- Affiliates are going to drive traffic to your Web site. Even if visitors do not purchase from you during their first visit, they may opt-in to your newsletter, if you have one, or add themselves to your subscriber list.

Questions to Ask

Now that you know the benefits of starting an affiliate program, is it for you? Setting up your own affiliate program is actually relatively simple, but there are several factors you need to take into consideration before you launch your affiliate program:

- Will your affiliates have a Web site that mirrors your own? Is each affiliate given a template of your Web site and a Web site address from which to promote your products?

- Will your affiliates earn commissions based on purchases only? Or do you also want to offer commission on the visitors they drive to your Web site based on clicks?

- What type of compensation will you offer affiliates: a commission of each sale (50 percent of each sale, for example) or a flat fee per sale? Keep in mind that if you search for affiliate programs, you will find that many offer a 50 percent commission and some offer as high as a 75 percent commission. The reason is simple: You have more people promoting your product or service, so your product or service is going to be exposed to far more people than it would if you were promoting it alone. Chances are you are going to make far more money, even offering a high commission, with your affiliates than you would promoting your product or service alone.

- Will you offer a one-tier or a two-tier affiliate program? A one-tier program is simply where you pay your affiliates for each sale that is made through their promotion. A two-tier program is "a type of affiliate program whereby affiliates earn commissions on the number of users they refer and convert. It also applies to the number of Web masters they refer and convert."

- Will you track each of your affiliates by assigning them a unique affiliate identification number?

- Do you have any restrictions on who can apply to be an affiliate? For example, can anyone anywhere be an affiliate or do you prefer only those who reside in the United States or in North America?

- What type of banners, if any, will you offer your affiliates to promote your products or services? Make sure you offer banners of different sizes, a convenience for your affiliate partners.

- Do you have a merchant account (we will discuss merchant accounts in the next chapter) by which you can track and pay affiliates? Or will you use a third party entity to keep track of and pay commission to your affiliates for you? (One such site is ClickBank – **www.clickbank.com**.).

Think about what you want to achieve with your affiliate program and answer each of the preceding questions before you do anything further.

Finding Affiliate Partners

Once you have decided the basics of your affiliate program, you will have to figure out how you are going to find affiliates to promote your products or services. There are several ways you can find affiliates:

- Add a "Become an Affiliate" link and page on your Web site, inviting your Web site visitors to apply to become an affiliate.

- Make the most of your signature line, both in your e-mails and when you post to message boards and forums, by including a link to your affiliate program information and sign-up page.

- List your product on ClickBank or Commission Junction (**www. cj.com**). Both are an excellent way for affiliates to find your product and sign on.

- Use Google's AdWords to advertise for affiliates.

- Find prospects you would like to have as affiliates and personally e-mail them to invite them to join your affiliate program.

After you market your affiliate program and have affiliates, cultivate relationships with those affiliates. Make their lives easier by informing them when a sale has been made through their promotion and send them e-mails from time-to-time updating them about your latest products or services. You may even want to consider offering them one of your products for free.

Ultimately, creating an affiliate program does take work, but the potential benefits far outweigh the time you will have to put into creating your banners and links (or outsourcing someone else to do it for you), setting up the program, and finding affiliates.

ADD A MESSAGE BOARD TO YOUR WEB SITE

Adding a message board to your Web site is surprisingly easy, especially if your Web host has the control panel.

If you decide to start a message board, make sure you or someone on your team moderates it and keeps an eye on the posting. Message boards are a haven for spammers, and if you do not have a moderator to delete the offensive posts and posters, you will find your board has more spammers than members.

The good news is, with most message board programs, you can ban IP addresses to ensure the spammers can no longer post from their IP address.

You can either use your message board as a standalone marketing tool or you can use it to build a online community. We will discuss message boards in-depth in the next section.

BUILD AN ONLINE COMMUNITY

There are thousands of online communities on the Internet. An online community allows likeminded people to congregate and share ideas, thoughts, news, and just to chat. Adding a message board, as we just discussed, is only the first step in building an online community. Many online communities feature message boards, chat rooms, and content (news, features, etc.).

Your first move should be to determine whether an online community is right for your Web-based business by answering the following questions:

- Do you have the time that it will require to build and maintain an online community? Even more important, do you have the desire to do so? If creating and maintaining an online community sounds like a pain or does not hold your interest, do not do it.

- Is your business niche conducive to group discussion?

- Do you think you can garner enough attention from your target market to build an online community that can flourish?

Answer those questions before you go any further. If you believe that an online community will benefit your Web-based business, you are ready to start building your online community.

Message Board/Bulletin Board

As we just discussed, a message board is easy to create and is an excellent platform for your customers. If you decide to use a message board, make sure you or someone you trust has the time to moderate the board.

As moderator of your message board, you have the ability to decide whether you want users to be able to register and immediately begin posting or if you want to approve each member before he or she can begin posting.

As was mentioned earlier, message boards are a haven for spammers, one of the reasons you must monitor your message board. You can delete the spammers' messages, and most message board programs allow you to ban IP addresses.

You will also want to create terms of service that outline what your message board members are allowed to do and what they are not allowed to do. For example, you may insist that no off color language be used, and you may provide a warning or two before the offender is banned.

You should also be aware of copyright laws when you run a message board. It is not uncommon for message board members to get into discussions and site online articles. However, in many instances, articles have copyrights which forbid copying content and placing it on another site. Your members should be made aware that copying content from an article could be violating copyright laws and instead of copying content, they should simply place a link to the article to which they are referring.

Your best bet would be to contact a lawyer to write the terms of service for you. If you do decide to write your own terms of service, have a lawyer look over it to make sure everything that should be included is included.

Many Web hosting companies offer the ability to create a message board quickly and easily — with little more than plugging in the extension you want for your message board URL (www.yoursite.com/messageboard, for example), choosing an admin name and password, and clicking the "install" button.

Chat Room

Unlike a message board, a chat room allows people to chat in real time. Some Web sites offer both message boards and chat rooms. There are numerous benefits to adding a chat room to your online community, including the ability for users to ask for advice or make comments and receive immediate feedback, if the chat room is a busy one.

The downside of the chat room, if you want to look at it that way, is the need for moderating it. If you do not have the time for moderating your chat room, you will likely want to find someone who can do so for you. Moderating your chat room allows you to weed out and ban the spammers and troublemakers.

A benefit of both message boards and chat rooms, if you create them through your Web host, is you own the message board or chat room; therefore, you can plug your products or services with posts, affiliate advertisements, and/ or your own ads. However, you want to be careful that you do not overrun your message board or chat room with blatant promotion, which could deter visitors from returning. Be subtle with your advertising.

Both a message board and a chat room will allow your customers to build camaraderie. It will also offer a venue for your customers to discuss your products or services, which in turn allows you to find out what they really think and where you can improve in some area of business.

Many Web hosting companies also offer the ability to create chat rooms. If you want to have a chat room on your Web site, make sure the host you choose allows you to create one.

Content

Most online communities are content rich sites. But you do not want just any content; make a concerted effort to provide content that both creates discussion among community members and informs your members about the latest news and information in your niche.

Do not just post content on your online community and forget about it. Update your Web site frequently with fresh content that is relevant to your niche and your target market.

As we discussed in Chapter 10, "Creating Powerful Content for Your

Web Site," you can either create content yourself or hire a professional writer to do it for you. If you are not a writer but decide to write your own content, proofread it before you post the content. It is also not a bad idea to proofread content if it is written by a professional writer or someone else.

Promoting Your Online Community

You need to draw people, customers, and potential customers, to your online community — one reason it is essential to provide a valuable resource. There are numerous ways to promote your online community, including:

- Join other online forums and discussion boards and start talking to people. Do not blatantly promote your online community. In some online forums and discussion boards, blatant promotion is prohibited. Get to know other people, become a valuable member, and promote your online community in your signature line (as long as you are allowed to do so, according to the particular forums terms of service).

- Announce your new online community to those subscribers who have opted-in for updates from your Web-based business or in your newsletter, if you send one out.

- Write a press release announcing your Web-based business's latest addition: your online community.

- Submit your online community's information to online community directories.

- Hold special events on your message board or in your chat room, and invite familiar names in your niche to participate in a question-and-answer session.

There is really no limit to how you can promote your online community, especially if you are creative.

Finally, creating and nurturing an online community will take hard work and commitment, but done right it will help your Web-based business gain valuable exposure and will likely help increase your sales.

Keep in mind that you do not have to start your online community immediately after you launch your Web-based business. You may want to wait until you have built a customer base, until you have time to properly devote to cultivating an online community, or until you have the funds to hire someone to do it for you. Regardless of who moderates and builds your online community, make sure you participate in it from time to time and offer tips or some nugget of valuable information. Getting to know your customers will show them you care about them and will help you gain valuable feedback.

OFFER E-COUPONS

You have numerous options when it comes to how and when you offer your customers e-coupons. And the only thing you need to generate e-coupons is a shopping cart that has coupon coding capabilities. (We will discuss shopping carts in-depth in Chapter Thirteen, "Merchant Accounts and Customer Payment Options.") When your customer decides to use a coupon, the only thing he has to do is, during checkout, type in the coupon code so the discount can be applied.

Your e-coupons may offer a discount on a particular item or a discount for the customer's overall purchase. Or you might want to offer an e-coupon that gives your customer free shipping.

There are a variety of ways you can offer e-coupons to your customers, including:

- You can use e-coupons to entice customers to sign up for your newsletter. You can also feature special e-coupons that are only available to newsletter subscribers.

- Offer your new, first-time customers e-coupons to encourage them to purchase your product or service.

- Keep track of your customers and send an e-coupon to those who have not purchased from you recently.

- Reward those customers who purchase from you again and again. You can do this by either offering periodic e-coupons as a "thank you" for frequently doing business with you or you can institute a customer loyalty program whereby customers receive e-coupons after they have been a customer for a certain period or have spent a certain amount of money purchasing from you.

- E-coupons are an excellent way to cross sell and upsell your customers. So if you sell printers, you might want to offer an e-coupon for customers who also purchase printer ink or printer paper.

You may come up with other promotional ideas with which you can offer e-coupons to your customers and potential customers. The key is to offer your customers e-coupons that entice them to purchase from you, whether for the first time or for the tenth time.

OFFER DISCOUNTS

Discounts are another way to thank your current clients for their business and to entice new clients to try your products or services. You must decide what type of discount to offer: Will you offer a discount for those who purchase your products or services in bulk? Will you offer a discount for those customers who purchase a particular product or service? Or will you offer a discount to all first time customers? Will you offer a dollar discount (i.e. $5 off your next purchase) or a percentage (i.e. 25 percent off all purchases over $100 or more)?

Once you know exactly what you are going to offer a discount for, you can announce it on your Web site, on your blog, and in your newsletter. State the terms of the discount clearly, so there is no misunderstanding on the customer's part.

HOLD CONTESTS

Get your customers and potential customers involved and drive more traffic to your Web site by holding contests. Contests are also a great way to attract publicity to your Web-based business, especially if your contest is unusually creative.

When deciding to hold a contest, keep several things in mind. First, offer a prize that has some value, something that your customers and potential customers really want. Of course, the prize should somehow have to do with your niche because that will naturally attract potential customers.

When deciding what type of prize to give away, make sure you can affordably deliver it anywhere in the world. Furthermore, the prize generally should not cost your business a lot of money.

Second, do not just offer a top prize. Rather, give prizes to the first and second runners up. Doing so will likely increase the number of entrants because people will likely think that they have better odds of winning, and they do.

E-MAIL/ONLINE NEWSLETTERS

Send out e-mail newsletters to customers who opt-in to receive them or publish an online newsletter. Newsletters are an excellent means of keeping in touch with your customers while also offering them valuable information they can use. Before we discuss the type of content generally found in newsletters, we will focus on the newsletter options you have. There are several types of newsletters from which you can choose.

Web Newsletter

A Web newsletter is a newsletter you publish on your Web site. Each week or month (however frequently you publish the newsletter), you will send an e-mail to customers who have opted in to remind them the latest newsletter is live.

Because the newsletter is published on a Web site, you can design it however you like — with as many photos, graphics, font types, colors, and so on — without having to worry about the restrictions of HTML and plain text e-mail newsletters.

Another upside to a Web newsletter is the opportunity to have your Web site listed and ranked in the search engines which, in turn, could drive more customers to your Web site. You can also create an archive for all of your past newsletters, making it easy for new subscribers to go back and read past issues.

Of course, nothing is ever perfect, and Web newsletters do have their downsides. First, if your customers decide to print out the newsletter, the printed version is going to pale in comparison to the onscreen version. Second, your subscribers must have an online connection or they simply will not be able to read the newsletter. Finally, whereas subscribers only have to open their e-mail to view and read their HTML or plain text e-mail newsletters, they will have to take the extra step to actually go to your Web site to view your newsletter. It is a small inconvenience, but an inconvenience nonetheless.

HTML E-mail Newsletter

E-mail newsletters are sent straight to the inbox of those customers who have opted in to receive them. HTML e-mail newsletters allow you to use graphics and photographs, and you can design and format the newsletter with different colors, fonts, and styles. HTML e-mail newsletters are often bold and creative, much like printed newsletters.

While HTML e-mail newsletters are a popular option, there are some disadvantages to using them. First, you may have some customers who simply cannot view the HTML newsletter because of the type of e-mail program they use. A solution to this, however, is to offer two versions of your newsletter — one in HTML and the other in plain text, and allow your customers to choose which they prefer when they opt-in to your subscriber list.

HTML e-mail newsletters may also take longer to download, depending on how many photos and graphics you use. If you do include photos and graphics, your subscribers will only be able to see the photos and graphics if they have an open connection to the Internet. While this will not likely be a problem for subscribers reading your newsletter from home, many employers today place heavy restrictions on their employees' Internet use. That means subscribers viewing your newsletter from work may not be able to see the photos and graphics.

Again, offering your customers the choice of receiving HTML or plain text e-mail is a positive way to solve this problem.

Plain Text E-mail Newsletter

Unlike HTML e-mail newsletters, plain text e-mail newsletters are simply that: only text. Plain text e-mail newsletters are very basic. You are unable to use different colors, different fonts, or any type of special formatting or design. It is, as the name implies, very basic.

The upside of using plain text is you will not have to spend a large amount of time worrying about formatting. Regardless of the type of e-mail your subscribers use, they will easily and quickly be able to read the newsletter. Of course, on the downside, plain text is, well, very plain, and you risk losing your readers' attention.

PDF Newsletters

PDF newsletters allow you to either send your newsletter to your subscriber list or publish it on your Web site as a download for your subscribers. Essentially, to create a PDF newsletter, you have to prepare the content and graphics in a Word document then transfer it to a PDF file. That means you have virtually unlimited creative freedom as to the type of design, fonts, colors, and graphics you use.

PDF newsletters are extremely popular with some organizations. For example, businesses like the Parkinson's Disease Foundation send out PDF newsletters to thousands of readers each quarter.

The biggest advantage of the PDF newsletter is if your subscribers want to print out the PDF newsletter, it will offer the highest quality compared to the Web newsletter, plain text e-mail, and HTML e-mail newsletters.

On the downside, PDF newsletters can take some time to download, especially if it is jam packed with photographs and graphics. If you plan to e-mail your subscribers the PDF newsletter, be aware of how big the PDF file actually is. Unfortunately, many e-mail programs limit how big a file can be, so if your file is too big, some of your subscribers may not be able to view it.

Additionally, if you opt for PDF format, to save space, you will likely have to ensure any photos are in a low resolution. That means if your subscribers print the newsletter out, the photos are going to be grainy and fuzzy.

Finally, for your readers to view a PDF newsletter, they will have to have Adobe Acrobat Reader on their computers which can be downloaded for free at **www.adobe.com/products/acrobat/readstep2.html**.

Deciding which type of newsletter to go with is a personal decision. You may want to experiment with one type of newsletter, see what type of response it receives, and keep using it if it works. If it does not work, you can always try another type of newsletter. Or you may want to conduct a survey to see what your customer base thinks and go with the majority.

If you opt to make a decision without input from your subscriber base, remember they are your target market. Choose the format you think would work best for them. Ask yourself the following questions: Are your subscribers likely to be Internet savvy? Are they the type that would prefer to print out the newsletter?

You also want to consider: Will your newsletter be free to your subscribers as a marketing tool? Or do you want to charge a fee? Many newsletters, used as a marketing tool, are free.

Newsletter Content Tips

Once you have decided the type of newsletter you are going to publish, you will need to decide on the type of content you want to offer your subscribers and how to make that content compelling and unique.

Start creating your content by sitting down and mapping out your first issue. Will you have a specific format you use each month? How many news articles will you have? Will you include a feature article? Having a specific format will allow you to know what space you need to fill each month, and your customers will also know what to expect each month.

Never Spam

The key with e-newsletters is to remember that you can never spam your e-mail list. Doing so is illegal, according to the CAN-SPAM Act of 2003. You must also ensure that you have an "Unsubscribe" link clearly stated in your newsletter. You may want to have it at the beginning and the end of your newsletter, making it easy for members to opt out.

To reiterate, the law states you must then take those recipients, who have requested you no longer send them e-mails, off of your list within ten business days. Failure to do so can result in hefty fines. You also want to ensure you do not share your subscriber list with any third parties unless you have specifically informed your subscribers that you will do so and they have, in return, given you permission to do so.

You may find that some people, regardless of how prominent the "Unsubscribe" link is, will simply hit the "Spam" button in their e-mail inbox. To deter such actions, you might want to include a note with the "Unsubscribe" link, emphasizing that opting out of your newsletter is easy and quick.

BLOG

A blog is a great marketing tool, and it is a great way to keep in touch with your customers and target market. You can either use a blog as part of your online community, or if you choose not to start an online community, your blog can be a standalone marketing tool.

As we discussed in the previous chapter, blogging is an effective and inexpensive way to market your business. If you decide to blog, make sure you offer your target audience content they can use and add to your blog frequently.

GIVE FREE SAMPLES

Everybody loves free samples. Think about it. The last time you were at your local shopping mall, walking through the food court, how many of the restaurants were handing out samples? How many times have you received samples of laundry detergent in the mail? If you have ever gone to a trade show, you have likely walked away with a bag full of samples. Samples are a great way to tantalize prospective customers by showing them how good your product or service is.

Say you sell your professional writing services through your Web-based business, and your target market is small business owners, with an emphasis on startups. Your Web site is professionally written, and you have even uploaded an online portfolio, so potential clients can see your writing style.

But, instead of simply offering potential clients examples of your writing, why not also offer them something that is of value to them and to their businesses? In our example, your target market is small businesses, and you also work with startups. For established small businesses, you might write a report on how to expand a business with aggressive marketing. For startups or those individuals considering taking the leap into entrepreneurship, you might decide to write a report on the ABC's of starting a business or marketing tips for building a loyal customer base.

Once you have written the report, you can post it for free on your Web site, in PDF format, or you might want to have a sign up box where the interested visitor types in his or her name and e-mail address. When you receive the request for the report, you send it. You can also have an autoresponder set up to send the report automatically.

By offering a free report, you are giving potential clients two things. First, you are giving them valuable information, a unique spin on a popular topic, something of value that they can incorporate into their businesses. Second, you are showing them the high quality of your work. You are giving them valuable information they can use, not some fluff that will cause them to click close on the PDF file after reading a few paragraphs.

If you are offering a product, you might also want to consider giving a free sample. For example, perhaps you sell homemade cookies to customers around the country, and you have decided to begin selling homemade candy, too. With every order of cookies, you might send a free sample of your famous chocolate bars to introduce your new candy selection to your customers.

If you can somehow offer your customers or potential customers a free sample, try it. If you do not see results, you can always stop offering the samples and try a different approach.

OFFER A BONUS

There is nothing better than purchasing a product or service and being surprised with a bonus. Consider offering your clients a bonus. Let us go back to the scenario in which you are a professional writer whose Web-based business offers résumé and cover letter writing services.

Perhaps you decide that with every resume and cover letter you sell, you will throw in a free, original thank you letter for clients to use after they have had interviews. The bonus gives your clients something valuable.

Or, if you want to take it a step further, you might offer a free half hour consultation with each client who orders a cover letter and resume package, to help prepare him or her for upcoming employment interviews.

If you are offering a bonus with a product, stipulate the conditions of the bonus. For example, you may want to limit the bonus to one per household. Say you are selling discounted airline tickets and your target market is recent college graduates and young adults who want to travel abroad. With every purchase, you might give away a free report or mini-book offering budget travel tips: from finding cheap accommodation to how to save money while still getting the most of your trip.

Whether you offer a product or a service, you have unlimited potential for offering a bonus as long as you are creative and think about what would be valuable to your customers.

BECOME A SPONSOR

Sponsor a local Little League, T-ball, or softball team. Provide the team players with their uniforms, including your business name on their shirts. Every time there is a game or a player wears his or her shirt away from the field, your Web-based business will get valuable exposure.

You may also want to sponsor a local radio or television show, which can bring you a lot of exposure and potentially drive a lot of traffic to your Web-based business.

PROVIDE SUPERIOR CUSTOMER SERVICE

How many times have you had a horrendous customer service experience? It probably leaves you with some negative feelings toward the company with whom you were dealing. One of the keys to your Web-based business's success and to building a loyal customer service base is providing superior customer service.

To ensure that your customers enjoy and benefit from their relationship with your business:

- Keep your promises. If you tell your client you will have a product or service to him by a specific date, make sure he has it before or on that date.

- Return phone calls promptly. Instead of having unanswered phone calls go to voicemail, have someone answer every phone call during your specified business hours. Try to return phone calls the same business day or the next business day, if possible.

- Answer e-mails quickly. As with phone calls, try to reply to e-mails the same business next or the next business day.

- Establish a refund policy. Clearly state your refund policy on your Web site, on your invoices, and on your receipts. Then adhere to that refund policy.

- Ask for feedback. Offer your customers the opportunity to tell you what they think by having a feedback form on your Web site or an e-mail address to which customers can send you their comments, suggestions, and complaints.

You may also want to compile a list of all of the customers who purchased from you during the month and e-mail them at the end of the month, thanking them for choosing your business and inquiring about their experience with you. Are they happy with the product or service they purchased? How was their experience with your customer service? Did they have an easy time finding what they wanted on your Web site? Was your Web site easy to maneuver? Make sure you also express that you are interested in their opinions and suggestions.

When a customer responds to your e-mail, take the time to write back and thank him or her for the feedback. The fact that you took the time to e-mail, not once but twice, will show your customers that you value what they have to say. In turn, chances are those customers will do business with you again…and again.

Dealing with Unhappy Customers

When you receive negative feedback, respond to it immediately, if possible.

You never want a client to harbor resentment toward you or your business. Addressing problems now, rather than later, is essential to retaining customers.

If your customer is not happy with a product, offer to refund the money immediately. If he is not happy with your service, ask him what you can do to fix the problem so he will be satisfied.

As much as you want to please your customers, remember that they are not always right. Try your best to solve the problem with your customer and to resolve his or her issue. But do not go overboard.

When all is said and done, however, you will deal with customers who are impossible to please during the life of your business. There will undoubtedly come a time when you will have to decide whether a customer's business is worth all the hassle. That is when you will ask: Should I fire this customer?

The time to fire a customer may have come if:

- Your customer simply does not trust you. For example, you are a Web designer and your client constantly has to "look over your shoulder" or micromanage you while telling you how to do your job. Some customers have to direct your every move because they are so worried you are going to make a mistake. As a result, you become physically and mentally drained from the stress of working with that client. Is the stress worth it to your business's bottom line?

- Your client is taking up a lot of your time. There are clients who feel it is necessary to call or e-mail the person they have contracted for a service or a product to determine the progress every hour. Ask yourself: Is the client taking up so much time it is not worth the business anymore?

- Your customer has a history of taking advantage of you. For example, your client insists he or she has an emergency and absolutely needs to get a press release written by the end of the business day, at which time he promises to pay you in full. You set aside other projects and rush to write the press release, but the client takes his or her time and waits several days to pay you. He or she does the same thing the next time he has a project he or she needs, and soon a pattern emerges. Is the hassle worth your time and the money you eventually earn from that client?

- Your client consistently pays invoices late. Things happen, and sometimes a client has no choice but to pay you late. However, if a client pays consistently late, you have a problem. Can you afford to keep such a client?

- Your customer is no longer willing to or can no longer afford your service rates or product prices and expects you to offer a lower price for that reason. Can you afford to keep this customer?

Firing a client is a business decision, and you should weigh the pros and cons of doing so. For example, if the client creates a huge portion of your income, is it really worth it to fire him or her? Can you find enough clients to fill the gap if you do fire him or her?

When you fire him or her, show him or her that the move is best for him or her. You may tell him or her, for instance, that your business is no longer capable of meeting his or her needs, and he or she would be much better off going with a different firm. Show the client that it benefits him or her to cease business with you. Never outwardly tell him or her you are getting rid of him or her.

A Postscript

As you can see, you have plenty of easy, inexpensive options for retaining your customers. In reality, you will likely devise numerous other creative ways to make it worthwhile for your customer base to return to you again and again and to attract new customers.

Building customer loyalty is essential to your Web-based business's ultimate success. Offering your customers effective, friendly customer support and giving them ways to get involved with your business — whether it is through contests, an online community, a newsletter, or asking for feedback — will show them you care about and appreciate their business.

13

MERCHANT ACCOUNTS AND CUSTOMER PAYMENT OPTIONS

Your Web site should be as consumer-friendly as possible, making it easy for customers to shop for and purchase your products or services. Transforming your Web site into a fully functioning store begins with finding a way for your customers to pay you for your products or services.

In this chapter, we will focus on how to apply for merchant accounts, the popular (and free) shopping carts that will make shopping on your Web site a breeze, and payment options with PayPal, Google, and eChecks.

How to Create a Merchant Account

A merchant account allows you to accept credit card payments directly from your clients, without using an outside service like PayPal or Google Checkout. If you want merchant status for each of the major credit cards — Visa, MasterCard, Discover, and American Express — you must apply for it. You can apply for merchant status directly with Discover and American Express only. For Visa and MasterCard, you must create a merchant account with a bank that establishes such accounts.

Those merchants who accept Discover Card pay only transaction fees and no monthly fees. Additionally, merchants have access to their accounts and to support 24 hours a day, seven days a week. Discover also offers their merchants the opportunity to process Visa, MasterCard, Diner's Club, and eChecks. To learn more or to fill out an application, visit Discover online at: **https://servicecenter.discovernetwork.com/msc/ exec/applyForm.do**.

Like Discover, you can apply for merchant status with American Express directly through the company itself. In addition to a complete "Merchant Account Guide," American Express allows its merchants to monitor their accounts for free and offers free marketing tools for business owners. To apply for merchant status with American Express, go to **https://home. americanexpress.com/homepage/merchant_ne.shtml**.

Visa and MasterCard are two of the most frequently used credit cards, so you will likely want to ensure your customers can pay with one or both of them. However, because Visa and MasterCard are bank associations, you will have to find a bank that offers merchant accounts to accept these credit cards.

Every bank has different requirements for approving merchant account applications, and some banks require an application fee. While most banks will not deny you based on the size of your business, you may have a more difficult time finding a bank that will give you a merchant account if you are a startup business.

Applying for a merchant account is akin to applying for a credit card or a loan: You must have good credit. If you have shaky credit, you are going to have a difficult time finding a bank that will approve you for a merchant account. If you are unsure of your credit score, get a copy of your credit report.

The three major credit bureaus are TransUnion (**www.transunion.com**), Experian (**www.experian.com**), and Equifax (**www.equifax.com**). Get a copy of your credit report, and check it for any errors, including any accounts listed as open that are really closed and debts that have been repaid but are listed as delinquent. Contact the credit bureaus to fix any errors. If you have credit problems, such as a past bankruptcy or a delinquent account, do not try to hide them. Rather, be upfront about your credit history.

Regardless of your credit score, you will have to provide the bank with detailed information, including your business plan, bank references, trade references, approximate volume of business you expect to do each month, and examples of your marketing materials.

When you apply for a merchant account, you are not simply filling out a piece of paper and waiting for approval or denial. You are presenting yourself and your business to your desired bank, so you want to be prepared and professional.

Finally, research different banks that offer merchant accounts to find the best bank for your needs. When deciding which bank best suits your business, take the following factors into consideration:

- What is the transaction fee for each credit card payment?

- What equipment is needed to process credit card payments?

- Are there fees for installing the needed equipment?

- What is the fee you will accrue for chargebacks?

- What are the monthly minimum fees if you have not met your sales?

- What is the discount rate (the percentage of each transaction that you will pay to the bank providing the merchant account)?

- If you have shaky credit, will you be required to pay any reserve fees that will protect the bank in case your business fails?

Having a merchant account that allows you to accept credit cards is only one of the steps in getting your Web site ready for customers. You will also have to consider how your customers will shop for your products or services. That is where e-commerce shopping carts come in.

SHOPPING CARTS

Much like the shopping carts consumers use at the grocery store, online shopping carts allow users to put in items they want to purchase and easily take those items out again if they change their minds. Essentially, a shopping cart is software that allows customers to browse through your merchandise, place what they want to purchase in the shopping cart, review their items for purchase, and purchase the items at the "checkout."

Many Web hosting packages offer shopping carts and implementing one can be as easy as installing it on your Web site. There are several popular shopping carts you can use to make your customers' purchasing experience quicker and easier.

Agora Shopping Cart

The Agora Shopping Cart is often included in Web hosting packages. If your Web host does not support Agora's Shopping Cart, you can download it for free at Agora's Web site (**www.agoracart.com**).

Agora's shopping cart supports such real-time shipping methods as UPS, the U.S. Postal Service, Federal Express, and Custom Shipping Options.

You can also add your Web site's URL to the AgoraCart Sites: a listing of those businesses that use Agora's shopping cart.

PayPal Shopping Cart

PayPal offers those PayPal clients with a premier or business account a free shopping cart that will allow them to easily receive credit card and bank payments from their customers. PayPal also allows you to create Buy Now buttons and provides support videos to help you install your shopping cart.

You can learn more about PayPal's shopping cart on the Web at: **www. paypal.com/cgi-bin/webscr?cmd=p/xcl/rec/sc-intro-outside**.

OS Commerce

Like Agora Shopping Cart and PayPal, OS Commerce is free software that will help transform your Web site into a virtual shopping center. OS Commerce supports such payment processors as PayPal, 2Checkout.com, ipayment, and payQuake. OS Commerce also allows for such payment methods as eCheck, money order, and credit cards.

If you opt to use OS Commerce, you can list your Web site's URL in their "Live Shops Directory." To learn more about OS Commerce or to download the software, go to: **www.oscommerce.com**.

PAYMENT OPTIONS

Once your customers have decided what to purchase and put the items in their shopping carts, they will need a way to pay for their purchases. Even if you have a merchant account and take credit card payments, not all of your customers will have credit cards. Therefore, it is important that you offer another way for customers to pay, and PayPal, Google Checkout, and eChecks are three of the most popular ways to do that.

PayPal

PayPal is an extremely popular payment option for both individuals and businesses. In addition to accepting the normal credit cards — Visa, MasterCard, American Express, and Discover — PayPal accepts eChecks as payment. PayPal allows merchants to create Buy Now buttons, offers chargeback support, gift certificates, and accepts multiple currencies.

PayPal also offers several payment methods for businesses, including:

- E-mail payments. With e-mail payments, you can invoice your customers via e-mail, and they can pay immediately via a bank transfer or a major credit card. You do not need a merchant account to accept e-mail payments, nor do you need a shopping cart. E-mail payments are currently free to set up and have no monthly fee. For a fee of $20 per month, you can use the Virtual Terminal, which allows your customers to pay by phone, fax, or mail.

- Web site Payments Standard. When your customer purchases a product or service from your Web site, he will then be redirected to PayPal's Web site to make the payment. When the payment has gone through, he will be taken back to your Web site. Setup is free; there are no monthly fees, and you do not need a merchant account. For $20 per month, you can use the Virtual Terminal.

- Web site Payment Pro differs from Standard in that the Virtual Terminal is included in the package, and there is a $20 monthly fee for the account. Setup is free, and customers can either pay for purchases on your Web site or you can redirect them to PayPal then back to your Web site.

- Payflow Gateway requires a merchant account. Customers can shop on your Web site and payment can be transferred from your online store to your chosen bank or payment processor. The Virtual Terminal is free. However, you will have to pay a setup fee (currently between $179 and $249) and a monthly fee ranging from $19.95 to $59.95 per month.

To learn more about PayPal, visit their Web site at: **www.paypal.com** and click on "Merchant Services." PayPal offers Live Chat support in addition to phone and e-mail support.

Google Checkout

The latest addition to the companies vying to help you accept payments is Google. Checkout allows business owners to do everything from charging customers' credit cards and processing orders to having the money transferred into the business owner's bank account. Google Checkout allows buyers to use their credit or debit cards — including Visa, MasterCard, American Express, and Discover — to pay for purchases. An added bonus of using Google Checkout is the fact that Google is waiving all transaction fees during 2007.

To be eligible to use Google Checkout, you must have a bank account and an address in the United States and either an EIN number/Federal Tax Identification *or* a valid credit card and a social security number.

Signing up for Google Checkout is simple and free. How long it takes to integrate Google Checkout into your Web-based business depends on what method of selling you choose:

• Buy Now. With the Buy Now button, your customers can simply click and purchase the items they want. Adding a Buy Now button to your products is simple and fast, depending on the number of products you are selling. Once the buttons are placed on your Web site, your customers can begin purchasing your products almost immediately.

- Off-the-shelf-shopping cart. If you are using a shopping cart that is compatible with Google Checkout, you simply have to plug in your Merchant ID and Merchant Key on your shopping cart's Web site.

- Custom shopping cart. If you want to develop your own shopping cart and integrate it with Google Checkout, you can. While it takes the longest of any of the methods of integration, Google provides a developer's guide you can use to create and integrate your custom shopping cart.

Google Checkout also works in conjunction with Google Adwords. When you use Google Adwords and Google Checkout, you can place a button denoting that you use Google Checkout. However, even if you do not use Adwords, you can still sign up for and use Google Checkout.

You can learn more about Google Checkout online at: **https://checkout. google.com**.

eCheck

eChecks are the online equivalent of, and work the same as, traditional paper checks. Many companies — including electric and gas companies — allow customers to pay their bills online through eChecks. When you use an eCheck, you are required to type in your routing number and bank account number before indicating the check's amount. In most cases, you have to retype your routing and account numbers to ensure you have not made any errors.

Because you cannot physically sign an eCheck, your eCheck is authorized with a digital signature. According to National Finance Center, a digital signature is "like a paper signature, but it is electronic. A digital signature cannot be forged. A digital signature provides verification to the recipient that the file came from the person who sent it, and it has not been altered since it was signed."

To offer your customers the option of paying by eCheck, you must have a bank with eCheck books and services.

There are a variety of benefits to offering your customers the option of using an eCheck. First, those customers who do not have a credit card can still purchase from you if they have a bank account.

eChecks are also convenient. You do not have to worry about receiving the traditional check in the mail, cashing it, and waiting for it to clear. Your customers do not have to spend time writing a traditional check, addressing the envelope, and mailing it to you.

Offering eChecks as a payment option also gives your customers a choice. Sometimes customers do not want to put more money on their credit cards, and by having the option of writing an eCheck, they do not have to.

14
ADDING A STOREFRONT

If you are going to be doing business on the Internet, you are going to need a virtual storefront that allows customers to browse your products, to put those items they want to purchase in a shopping cart, and to proceed to checkout where they will make their final purchase.

Some businesses create their own virtual storefronts while others, who either do not have the time or the funds to devote to building an e-commerce Web site from scratch, turn to already established e-commerce sites to quickly, affordably, and easily build their virtual storefronts.

There are a variety of well-known, popular businesses that allow business owners to create virtual storefronts, including eBay, Yahoo, and Amazon. The beauty of creating a virtual storefront through such a venue is the fact that you are not limited to having a storefront just through Yahoo. You can build one through eBay, Yahoo, and Amazon, if you want to really increase your exposure.

eBay Storefront

eBay is undoubtedly the most popular online auction marketplace on the Internet, and people sell everything and anything on eBay. Thousands of entrepreneurs have even gone on to establish their own full-time and part-time businesses selling through eBay.

While eBay can be incredibly profitable, it is the same as any business: It requires time and hard work. Still, as an eBay seller you do not have to worry about building your own e-commerce Web site.

The first step in creating an eBay storefront is knowing how eBay's auctions work. There are several ways you can sell your items through eBay: standard auction, reserve auction, multiple-item auction, or fixed price Buy It Now.

- When you run a standard auction, you place an item on eBay for sale and designate a starting bid amount. The starting bid generally ranges from one dollar to $1.99, and the highest bidder wins the auction. You set the auction's duration.

- When you set a firm price that must be met for a purchase to be completed, you are opening a reserve auction. Until someone bids the reserve price, no bidders actually know what that price is: Only once someone's bid meets or exceeds the reserve price, the reserve price is unveiled to all bidders.

- Multiple item auctions are simply those auctions in which you sell several of the same items. Again, you would set a minimum bidding price, and the bidders with the highest bids win, depending on how many items are for sale. (For example, if two items are for sale, the two highest bidders would win the auction.)

- When you offer fixed-price buy it now products, you set a specific price for an item. A buyer then pays that fixed price, and the item becomes his or hers.

One of the keys to success as an eBay seller is to build strong feedback. When a buyer purchases from you, he is then able to rate the transaction as positive, neutral, or negative and to comment on exactly what he thought about the experience.

As a way to instill trust in your buyers, before you build your feedback, create an "About Me" page. The page is free to all eBay sellers and gives you the opportunity to establish your business identity, inform buyers what products you sell, and include links to those products in your eBay storefront. You can even include a picture of yourself if you want.

In addition to building strong feedback to instill trust and loyalty in buyers, you must also get them excited about buying from you with photographs and vivid descriptions of the products you are selling.

To start your own eBay storefront, go to **www.ebay.com**.

Yahoo Small Business

Formerly known as Yahoo Store, Yahoo Small Business allows business owners to quickly set up, using a storefront design wizard, and establish a storefront. If you would rather not use the design wizard, you will be allowed access to Yahoo's recommended storefront developers.

Yahoo Small Business charges both a monthly fee and a transaction fee for each transaction. How much you pay and exactly what features you get depends on which of the three monthly packages you choose:

- The Starter Package has far less in terms of features and benefits, but Yahoo recommends it for those businesses that anticipate earning less than $12,000 per month. The Starter Package has the highest transaction fee, currently set at 1.5 percent.

- The Standard Plan, which is recommended if you anticipate selling between $12,000 and $80,000 per month, allows you to offer your customers coupons and gift certificates, while keeping track of your sales through a trails report. The current transaction fee for the Standard Plan is 1 percent.

- If you anticipate selling more than $80,000 per month, you will likely want to sign up for the Professional Plan, which offers the same features and benefits of the Standard Plan with a .75 percent transaction fee.

As your business grows, you can easily upgrade to the next package level. Those who subscribe to the Standard and Professional packages receive myriad of benefits, most notably access to Customer Support 24/7 and full shopping cart capabilities. Yahoo also provides 60 days of consulting while business owners set up their storefronts.

To learn more about Yahoo Small Business, go to: **http://smallbusiness. yahoo.com/ecommerce**

Amazon Storefront

After offering an affiliate program for more than a decade, Amazon expanded its reach by offering their affiliates the opportunity to create their own virtual storefronts — aStore — making it easy to sell Amazon's products and make a commission.

All affiliates — known as Associates with Amazon — can build an aStore for free and choose products from Amazon that they want to feature in that store. You must first sign up as an associate, which you can do online at: **http://affiliate-program.amazon.com/gp/associates/join**.

Associates generate a commission of up to 8.5 percent, a much smaller commission than you would be paid if you promoted an individual product from ClickBank, for example. However, with Amazon's aStore, you can promote an entire store of products at once. Additionally, Amazon offers a commission only on qualifying purchases, so make sure you promote only those products on which you will earn a commission. You will be paid quarterly for any commissions you earn.

Creating an Amazon aStore can literally take only minutes, and you can have your aStore go live immediately after creating it. To learn more about aStore, visit: **http://astore.amazon.com**.

15

HIRING EMPLOYEES

There may come a time when you are so busy with your Web-based business and your business is growing so fast that you need help. You have two choices when it comes to finding help: You can either hire an employee or employees or you can engage the services of an independent contractor.

If you decide to hire an employee or employees, you should know what to expect from the entire process: from the interview to the end of that employee's stint with your Web-based business. This section focuses on preparing you for working as a manager and for hiring employees.

General Management Skills

Knowing how to manage your business is vital to your success; it is also essential to the success of your employees. If you are like many small business owners, you likely have some level of apprehension about hiring employees or independent contractors to take over some of the business tasks. After all, you know how to run your business better than anyone. In this section, we will discuss ways to run your business efficiently while also effectively managing your employees.

Successfully running and managing your Web-based business requires you to be a leader, not a follower. As a leader, your role is multi-dimensional.

First, you must remain informed about the latest news and information in your particular niche or industry. That means you might have to set aside time each day or week to read industry publications or to network with others in your industry. Knowing what is going on is vital to ensuring your Web-based business gets ahead, and stays ahead, of the competition.

Second, you have to realize that you cannot do everything. If you try to take responsibility for everything that needs done, you are only going to work long hours that will eventually lead to burnout. Therefore, you must learn how to delegate.

Delegating responsibility requires careful thought. Rather than just assigning certain tasks to specific employees, take the time to assess your strengths and weaknesses, as well as your employees' strengths and weaknesses. Delegate those tasks, where your skills are the weakest, to an individual who has strong skills in that area. For example, if you are weak at writing advertisements, delegate that responsibility to an employee who has strong writing skills.

To ensure that your employees know exactly what their responsibilities are, create a procedure manual that details, step-by-step, each of the responsibilities and how they are to be executed. For example, if you have an employee who is in charge of answering customer inquiries by e-mail, write exactly what you expect the employee to do, including: frequency of checking e-mails (every hour, every half an hour, etc.), time of turnaround (answer all e-mails within an hour of receiving during business hours or 12 hours during non-business hours), etc.

Thoroughly documenting each task will help you in several ways. First, it will allow you to concentrate on your responsibilities while knowing that your employees know exactly what they are supposed to do. Second, your employees will know exactly what they need to do which, in turn, means you will have more time to concentrate on your own responsibilities. Having tasks outlined on paper means employees will ask you far fewer questions while still being able to do their job to the best of their abilities.

Third, you must be able to make decisions, sometimes in a split second. Learning how to make decisions quickly is much easier than it sounds. There are several things you can do to ensure that you make the best decisions for your business.

To begin, consider the situation that requires a decision and ask yourself the following questions: Is it necessary that I make decision regarding this situation? How quickly does the decision need to be made? Who will this decision affect?

If you have time to make a decision, research your choices and the consequences of each choice, and create a list of alternative choices. Remember, however, that there will be times you will have to make decisions quickly.

Fourth, effective time management is key to your success as a business owner. Trying to do everything in one day is a recipe for disaster: You will likely be stressed and get less done. Instead of trying to get everything done in one day by yourself, plan your time to ensure you maximize your working hours.

Creating, and following, a time management plan is the first step to taking control of your time. Before you can sit down and write your plan, however, you need to do two things. First, you have to determine where you are wasting time during your day. For example, how much time do you spend during your workday checking or answering personal e-mail? How much time do you spend surfing the Internet? How long do you spend on personal phone calls or chatting with friends?

To identify those non-work related activities that are costing you time, track your activities for several days, making note of how you spend your time. After you have tracked your activities, you can sit down and literally see where your time is being wasted.

After you have identified time wasting activities, you can then set time management goals. Your goal may be to alleviate stress or you may want to accomplish more during your workdays. Whatever your goal, write it down and keep it in mind as you work toward better managing your time.

In addition to setting time management goals, you can better manage your time by doing several simple things:

- Prioritize your tasks. Know what you need to accomplish each day by taking the time to list what needs to be done in order of urgency. You can create your priority list either in the morning before you start working or the night before.

- Set a routine. With a routine, your workday will flow, and you will know what you need to get done and when. For instance, you probably check your e-mail several times a day. When you create a routine, designate specific times to check your e-mail: once in the morning, right after lunch, and at mid-afternoon, for example. If you follow it, a routine allows you to better manage your time by knowing what you are going to do and when throughout your work day.

- Get organized. There is no bigger time waster than disorganization. Organize your office and your files. For example, how long does it take you to find files you need to work with on your computer? If you are organized, you likely have each project you are working on categorized in separate folders, which makes it easy for you to find exactly what you need in mere seconds. If you are not organized, you likely spend several minutes, if not more, searching for the file with which you need to work. Even though it may only take you three or four minutes to find your file, add those minutes up throughout the workday, and you are wasting considerable time, which could be spent more productively.

- Take advantage of time management tools. In today's high tech world, there are plenty of ways to stay organized and to better manage your time. Take advantage of the time management tools available to you. For example, if you have a Windows-based computer, you probably have Microsoft Outlook. In addition to allowing users to send and receive e-mail, Outlook offers numerous time management benefits, including a calendar that will remind you of important tasks or meetings and a To-Do bar that allows you to list all of your daily responsibilities.

Ultimately, you can eliminate the stress in your work life and accomplish what you want on a daily basis by taking control of your time and better managing it.

Employees

There is more to hiring and having employees than just choosing the best candidate for the position and hiring him. You must know what interview questions are legal and which are illegal. You must know how to handle applicants you are not going to hire, and you must know how to manage employees. This section focuses on what you need to know to hire, manage, and terminate your employees.

The Employee Interview

The employee interview is just as important for your candidates as it is for you, so treat each interviewee with the utmost respect and professionalism. Sure, you might have a few applicants that simply are not a good match for the job, but maintain professionalism. After all, each applicant is also a potential customer.

To ensure the interview process goes smoothly, be fully prepared and ready to meet with the applicants:

- Arrive for the interview on time, so you do not leave your applicants waiting. Alternately, if you are interviewing applicants over the phone, call the applicant at the agreed upon time. Arriving or calling late or switching interview times may leave your applicants with an unfavorable impression of you and how you run your Web-based business.

- Write a detailed description of the job you are offering. You must know the exact responsibilities that the position requires, so you can adequately determine which applicants are qualified for the position.

- If you are conducting the interview in-person, do so in a private place and let others know that you are not to be disturbed. Likewise, if you are interviewing over the phone, do not answer call waiting and interrupt your interview. Keep any interruptions to a minimum.

- Engage the applicants and help them to feel at ease. For an in-person interview, sit in comfortable chairs and consider offering applicants a glass of water or something else to drink. After all, applicants can often be nervous, and it may be an appreciated gesture. During the interview, keep your tone conversational and show interest in what the applicant is saying.

- Schedule enough time for each interview and be open to applicant questions. After all, when you advertise for a job, you generally have limited space in which to describe the job, pay, and other important issues. Be prepared for, and encourage, questions.

- Allow applicants to talk, when possible. You can learn a lot about applicants, especially when they talk about themselves, their previous jobs, their former employers, and their experiences in school. Listen carefully and make a mental note of any inconsistencies and excuses. Another red flag to watch for is the applicant becoming negative or speaking negatively. Another clear indication of a problem is an applicant who tries to avoid the subject at hand. Rather than aggressively persisting to find out the real story, go on with your questions. But go back to the question and do what you can, without being overbearing, to get the whole story.

- Even if you are not open-minded, do what it takes to appear that way. An applicant may have done or said something of which you disapprove, but do not let him or her know that. But you certainly do not want to approve or condone behavior or words that are blatantly wrong.

- Ask questions that will give you a chance to see how the applicant responds to unexpected questions, such as: What do you like to do to relax? What are your hobbies? What is the last book you read? Asking such questions will also help you get a feel for the applicant's personality, attitude, and energy level.

Prepare a list of questions beforehand, so you do not miss anything. One of the best questions you can ask is: What did you like best about your previous job? Are the things that the applicant mentions similar to those responsibilities he will have if you hire him or her?

Include on your list of questions, an inquiry that is behavior-based. For example, if the job applicant is applying for a customer service position that includes answering questions on the phone, ask him something like, "What would you do if an irate customer calls and demands you fix her problem?" Or, "How would you react if a customer is not happy with how you have handled the problem and asks to speak to the person in charge?"

Unlawful Pre-Employment Questions

According to the law in the United States, there are some questions are illegal. In this section, you will be provided with an overview of those questions and how to avoid them. However, you should not use this section as a replacement for legal advice. If you are unsure about something, consult an attorney.

In fact, you should set aside time to discuss unlawful pre-employment questions with not only your attorney but also with your state and federal labor offices. You can either have your attorney write standard employment applications or you can purchase them from your local office supply store. If you decide to purchase the applications from an office supply store, you should have your lawyer look at the application to ensure there are no illegal questions, either stated or implied.

According to the Federal Civil Rights Act of 1964, as well as other federal and state laws, job applicants are to be treated fairly and equally, regardless of race, color, age, religious creed, national origin, or sex. To adhere to these regulations, you are not legally allowed to ask certain questions that pertain to the previously mentioned categories. You must be aware of the very fine line between illegal and legal questions applicants may be asked.

When you create a list of questions, you should use common sense. Asking an illegal question will not have any bearing on whether or not you hire the applicant anyway. Always steer clear of any questions that will infringe upon or are related to an applicant's civil rights.

Age and knowing an applicant's date of birth only comes into play when the business holds liquor, beer, or wine licenses. Otherwise, age is a very sensitive subject. The Age Discrimination in Employment Act was passed to protect employees over the age of 40. You can read the full act at **www. eeoc.gov/policy/adea.html**. You are allowed to ask an applicant his age if he is under 18. There are times when you will need an applicant's date of birth for such internal reasons as a profit-sharing plan or starting a pension, but that comes after you hire an applicant.

You are legally allowed to ask an applicant if he or she smokes or uses drugs. One of the benefits of the application is your ability to obtain the applicant's agreement that he will be legally bound to the employer's smoking and drug policies.

More Problematic Pre-Employment Questions

If you ask an applicant if he or she knows people who work with the company, you must be careful that you do not give that applicant preferential treatment. Other problematic pre-employment question areas include:

- **Credit history or credit rating** — Both have been deemed discriminatory against both women and minorities.

- **Home ownership** — Home ownership questions have been ruled discriminatory, especially against minorities because many do not own homes.

- **Military discharge** — While you can ask questions about an applicant's military experience and/or training, you are not allowed to ask about the type of discharge the applicant received. Such questions have been ruled improper because of the proportionally high less-than-honorable discharge rates of minorities.

- **Disabilities** — According to The Americans with Disabilities Act, you are forbidden to ask general questions about health problems, medical conditions, and disabilities.

Following is a list of some questions you are prohibited by law to ask of applicants. While some may be blatantly obvious, it is important to mention them nonetheless.

- What color are your eyes?

- How tall are you?

- Do you go to church? If so, which one?

- Do you or does anyone you know have HIV?

- How old are you?

- Have you ever been in prison?

- Are you really a man/woman?

- Do you regularly work out at the gym?

- Do you own or rent your home?

- Are you a minority?

- Is English your first language?

- Are you Japanese or Chinese?

- Have you declared bankruptcy in the past?

- Where are your parents from?

- Have you ever received worker's compensation from a previous employer?

- If you get this job, who will take care of your children?

- How many times have you been married?

- Are you gay?

- How does your boyfriend or girlfriend feel about you working with this company?

- Are you currently in a committed relationship?

Screening Job Applicants

By screening job applicants, you will better be able to reject those applicants who are not suited for working with your business prior to asking them to return for an even lengthier interview. If you are a one-man operation at this point, you will find that this saves you both time and money.

When applicants leave the interview or hang up the telephone, they should feel as though they were treated fairly and were presented with an equal opportunity to show you why they are the ideal candidates for the job. Even if you know applicants are not right for the position, treat them well. After all, they may very well be future customers.

The following criterion is a good place to start with your preliminary screening:

- **Experience.** Does the candidate have the qualifications to do the job? Analyze the applicant's job experience, and check all of his references.

- **Appearance.** Was the candidate neatly dressed? This probably is not a big consideration if the open job is for a position that does not require the applicant to appear in public. However, a neatly dressed applicant — regardless of the position — shows that he or she is serious about the job and making a good impression.

- **Personality.** Does the applicant have a personality that will fit in with your Web-based business?

- **Legality.** Does the candidate meet all of the legal requirements?

- **Availability.** Can the applicant work the hours you need?

Each applicant's application must be signed and dated. Once you have gone through the first round of in-person or telephone interviews, you will want to split all applicants into three categories:

- Refer the applicant. If someone else will be conducting the second interview, you refer the applicants who you think are best for the position.

- Reject the applicant. Write on the application the exact reasons for the applicant's rejection and put the application in a file. You never know: It may come in handy in the future.

- Put the applicant in the prospective file. Some of the candidates may not be qualified for the position you are currently offering. So start a prospective file for applicants you would like to consider if you need help in other areas of your Web-based business in the future.

Qualities to Look for in Potential Employees

If you are going to hire an employee or employees to work for your Web-based business, you will have to consider one thing: Will the employee(s) work on site or will the employee work from home? The following are qualities you want to look for in employees who are going to work for your Web-based business both onsite or from home, but some are even more important for home-based positions.

- **Self-discipline**. Self-discipline is required for any position, but if your employee is going to work from home, it is absolutely critical. There are a lot of distractions when working from home. Does the applicant have the self-discipline it takes to work remotely?

- **Determination.** Does the applicant have determination and does he or she finish what he or she starts? Or does he or she fall into a pattern of starting but not finishing? Analyze the applicant's employment and school history

- **Independence**. Is the applicant independent? Does the applicant live on his or her own or with his or her parents? Do you know how old the applicant was when he or she moved away from home? Why did he or she leave home? Independence is critical, especially for those who are going to be working remotely or with little direct supervision.

- **Motivation**. Find out why the applicant wants to work for your Web-based business. Does he or she hope to learn and grow with the business or is the position simply a stepping stone to something else? Is the applicant motivated from within or does he or she find motivation in dominating others?

- **Stability**. Does the applicant stick with jobs or does he or she stay for only a few months before moving on? Check out his or her employment history to find out how long he or she has worked at previous jobs. You do not want to hire someone who has a penchant for quitting a job every few months.

- **Maturity**. Is the applicant mature? Does he or she have what it takes to work with minimal or no direct supervision?

- **Work habits.** Does the applicant have strong work habits? This is a question former employers should be able to answer well. Does the applicant need a lot of supervision or can you give him or her a project and he will run with it? If your employee is going to be working from home, you must determine whether he or she has the strong work habits that are needed for working independently.

Deciding Who to Hire

By this point, you should have several candidates who are suitable for the position. Making the final selection is often the hardest part of the entire process. In all likelihood, you have several applicants with topnotch qualifications who would be ideal for the position, but now you have to decide who the best candidate for your Web-based business is.

You should make your decision based on what you learned about the applicant through his or her interview, application, résumé, and references. If you had someone else also interview the applicants, ask that person for his or her recommendation. Which applicant stands out in his or her mind? Why?

Even if the employee(s) will work from home, you have to make sure he is someone with whom you are comfortable working and relying on, and someone whom you believe can do the job and do it well.

When you have made your decision, you will be ready to offer him or her the job. Be sure that you explain in detail each of the following, and the applicant understands the terms and conditions of his or her employment before he or she agrees to accept the position:

- **Job Description.** Explain the exact responsibilities the applicant will have in the position, what hours he or she is expected to work, what you expect from him or her as an employee, and at what physical location he or she will work (at home or at your office).

- **Work Details.** Inform the employee of the time and date of his or her first day on the job.

- **Salary.** Ensure the applicant knows his or her starting rate of pay, whether he or she will be paid hourly or on a salary, any benefits offered, health insurance offered, and vacation and personal days.

Rejecting Applicants

No one likes rejection, and that makes rejecting applicants both a difficult and an unpleasant necessity. The good news is the majority of the applications you receive, you will reject almost immediately. You will find there are those applicants who want to know why they are being rejected.

While you want to be honest, do so in a tactful manner. The last thing you want is to initiate a confrontation, so briefly explain why the application is being rejected. An acceptable response would be, "We've extended an offer to an applicant with more experience…" or "We offered the position to a better qualified candidate."

If you have decided to put the candidate's application in your prospective file, you may want to tell the candidate you have done so. However, you should avoid giving the applicant the impression that there is a good chance you are going to hire him or her in the future, and you certainly do not want to mention a specific date when you will be looking for a new employee.

Your Employee Handbook and Personnel Policies

Even if your Web-based business only has one employee, you are required by federal law to have written policy guidelines for your employee(s). An employee handbook or policy manual helps new employees understand a business's policies and procedures, and it also provides management with a guide as to how things are supposed to be done.

To reiterate, regardless of the size of your business or the number of employees, you must have an employee handbook or policy manual. Such a handbook has numerous benefits, among them:

- Having your policies and procedures written down could keep you from having to go to court should a dispute or a problem arise.

- You will be able to prevent misunderstandings and problems.

- You can save time. Rather than answering each new employee's questions, you can refer him or her to the employee handbook. You can then answer any questions he or she still has, after reading the handbook.

- Your Web-based business, no matter how big or how small, appears professional to your employee(s).

- The implementation of an employee handbook has been proven to not only increase employee productivity but also employee compliance and retention.

At the heart of many workplace legal disputes is a lack of communication and inadequate policies and guidelines. The failure of employers to inform employees of the business's standard policies and procedures, unfortunately, has resulted in millions of dollars in subsequent legal judgments. If you do not inform your employees of the policies and guidelines and an employee is fired for breaking a rule, you may face a lawsuit. In fact, many terminated employees have successfully used the defense of not knowing the policies and procedures.

After your employee reads the employee handbook, make sure he or she signs and dates a statement that says he has received, read, understands, and will comply with all of the policies and guidelines in the handbook.

Writing an employee handbook is a time consuming process, but it is an essential step for you to take. Otherwise, you open yourself up to potential lawsuits.

Following are the topics you should cover in your employee handbook:

- Standards of Conduct
- Employee Conduct
- Bonus Plans
- Insurance
- Absenteeism
- Company Vehicles
- Punctuality
- Personal Appearance
- Work Performance
- Confidentiality
- Performance Reviews
- Safety

- Work Area Neatness
- Availability for Work
- Personal Mail and E-mail
- Personal Telephone Calls
- Benefits Program
- Eligibility for Benefits
- Mandatory Meetings
- Communication
- Problem Resolution
- Disciplinary Guidelines
- Employee Relations
- Harassment
- Employment References
- Personnel Files
- Pre-Tax Deductions
- Military Leave
- Rehiring Employees
- Solicitation
- Substance Abuse
- Contributions
- Company Property

- Weapons Policy
- Violence
- Severe Weather
- Holidays
- Vacation
- Bereavement Leave
- Workplace Monitoring
- Orientation
- Suggestions
- Criminal Convictions
- Social Security
- Employment of Relatives
- Outside Employment
- Social Security
- Personal Property Searches
- Employee Discounts, if applicable
- Hours of Work
- Workers' Compensation
- Employment Classification
- Recording Time
- Jury Duty

- Office Equipment
- Family Leave of Absence
- Tools and Equipment
- Job Abandonment
- Voluntary Resignation
- Payroll
- Break Policy
- Termination Procedures
- Overtime
- Travel Expenses

- Educational Assistance
- Reimbursable Expenses
- Salary and/or Wage Increases
- Acts of Misconduct
- Other Forms of Separation
- Equal Employment Opportunity
- Affidavit of Receipt
- Unemployment Compensation
- Performance-Based Release
- Medical Leave of Absence

If you cannot afford to hire a professional to write your employee handbook, make sure you create one yourself and have your attorney view it.

The Employee File

After you have hired a candidate, you want to immediately create an individual employee file that contains the following information:

- The employee's application.
- A W-4.
- The employee's social security number.
- The employee's legal name, address, and phone number.
- Emergency phone number(s) for the employee.
- Date employment has commenced.
- Job title.

- Rate of pay.

- Current and previous performance evaluations.

- Signed and dated statement acknowledging that the employee has read and accepts the terms of the employee handbook/policy manual.

- You will also include a termination date, if the employee leaves, and a detailed reason for why the employee has been terminated.

Tips for Training

Depending on your Web-based business's employee needs, you may need to train your employees. The most effective way to approach training is to think of it not as employee training but as employee development. Emphasize that employee development is an investment for them and for you. Employee development, of course, is an ongoing process that continues as your employees learn and grow with your business.

Employee development is essential to not only the growth of your business and the growth of your employees but also to overall employee satisfaction and employee loyalty. According to SCORE, those businesses that offer their employees growth opportunities often have employees that are more likely to be satisfied and, in turn, to remain with their respective companies.

When you train your employees, make sure they know why you are training them and exactly how the training is going to benefit them and their contributions to the business. To achieve this goal, you need to be prepared before you begin training. Having a specific purpose will help you better focus your training sessions.

You will also need to determine:

- Where are you going to hold the training sessions? In the office? If your employees work remotely, will you rent a conference room at the local hotel or do you prefer to hold the training in an online environment? Whichever location you ultimately choose, make sure it is both spacious and conducive to learning.

- Who is going to conduct the training? Will you do it yourself as the owner of your Web-based business? Or will you hire someone from outside?

- When will you conduct the training? Will you do it during your employees' normal work hours or will you do it after business hours or on the weekend? The law requires that you pay your employees for training, a factor you might want to consider when deciding when to hold training sessions.

- What do you expect to result from the training? What employee changes do you hope will result from the training? You must answer this question for yourself and for your employees. Before you begin a training session, tell them what changes you expect to see.

- What types of materials are you going to use for the training session? Handouts help emphasize important points and can be used as a refresher for employees in the days and weeks after the training session.

Employee training and development does not end after your training sessions. It is an ongoing process, one you have to continually monitor and improve upon. Determine if the changes you wanted were actually made.

Evaluating Employee Performance

Regardless of the size of your Web-based business, you will want to perform periodic employee performance evaluations. To ensure you provide the fairest evaluation possible, keep in mind the following tips:

- Make sure you thoroughly understand your employee's job description and what you expect from him. Remember, your goal is to evaluate the individual employee's performance, not stack him or her up against other employees. You also should not judge your employee based on what you think his or her potential is.

- Regardless of whether you are conducting the evaluation in-person or over the phone, make sure you do so in a private place where you will not be interrupted. If you are evaluating more than one employee on the same day, give yourself plenty of time for and between each evaluation, so you do not have to rush.

- Keep an open mind during the evaluation, and do not focus on only one situation or characteristic, regardless of whether it is positive or negative. Rather, consider the entire period since the employee's previous evaluation.

- Start the evaluation on a positive note by focusing on the good aspects of the employee's performance, then ease into the discussion of the areas in which the employee needs to improve.

- Do not allow an evaluation to become one-sided. You do not want to focus 100 percent on the negative, but you also do not want to focus completely on the positive. If your employee is not living up to your expectations, you are certainly not going to motivate him or her with an entirely negative evaluation. Mention some of the employee's positive traits and contributions before thoroughly discussing the improvements that should be made. An entirely negative evaluation will also frighten your employee. If an employee honestly warrants only negative comments, you should probably consider terminating that employee.

- Take time to go over previous evaluations; however, refrain from dwelling on them. You want to keep an eye out for areas where your employee has either improved or declined since his or her last performance evaluation.

- During the evaluation, backup all of your comments and claims with examples, and allow the employee to rebut and speak as long as necessary. In some instances, you may remember a situation wrong. Allow the employee the time to refute your claims. If you do provide examples on issues you have never discussed with the employee, you have let the communication lag.

- Your employee is not going to change overnight, so do not expect it. Remember, improvement is a gradual process, and the evaluation is only one step in that process.

- Do not go over too much during the evaluation or you may overwhelm your employee.

- There are certain things — like deficiencies and personality traits — that cannot always be changed. Do not harp on these aspects, but illustrate to the employee how these traits may affect both his or her performance on the job and co-workers' performances.

- Always end the evaluation on a positive note. You want your employee to feel confident about his or her overall performance, but also to realize that there are areas in which he or she can and should improve. You should make clear the steps he or she should take to improve.

- Several days or a week after the evaluation, follow up with your employee and go over the ideas and recommendations that were discussed during the evaluation. Rather than enhancing and reinforcing the evaluation, failure to do this will only make the evaluation useless in the long run.

Finally, keep all of your employee evaluations confidential. If you keep the evaluations in individual employee files, make sure no one else has access to those files.

Legally Firing an Incompetent Employee

Unfortunately, not all employees work out. That is a fact of business. There will come a time when you will decide that the best thing to do is to terminate an incompetent employee. Before you decide to let an employee go, however, you should give him or her a fair evaluation and a chance to raise his or her standard of work. If that does not happen, you are ready to let him or her go.

Terminating an employee is never fun, and it can often be one of the most difficult tasks you will face. But terminating an ineffective employee will ultimately be the best move for your business.

Before you decide to terminate your employee, have you considered retraining him or her for the position? Sometimes retraining will work, and sometimes it will not. Do not make the decision to terminate an employee when you are tired, angry, or stressed. Wait until you are calm, and you can be as objective as possible. Weigh both the pros and the cons of the employee's performance.

If the employee has a supervisor, talk with that supervisor to evaluate the employee and the situation as a whole. Review the employee's training, his or her supervision, and his or her previous evaluations. Consider: Have you or have the employee's other superiors in some way caused, contributed to, or even perpetuated the problem? You also want to ask whether the employee has had an opportunity to improve his or her performance. If not, he or she should have a fair opportunity to improve.

Once you have made the decision to terminate the employee, schedule a meeting with him or her. You should schedule the meeting immediately, and do not let more than 24 hours pass before you talk with the employee. You do not want others to learn what is happening until you have talked to the employee.

If you are not the employee's direct supervisor, the direct supervisor should also be at the exit interview for two reasons. First, he or she will be able to support you as you terminate the employee. Second, he or she will be a witness as to how the exit interview went. Having a witness is crucial because the employee may attempt legal action to ensure he or she gets a settlement.

Exit interviews should be conducted in a private room where you will have no interruptions. Your employee may disagree with some of the points you make. Allow him or her to refute your claims, but you must ensure you have statements and proven facts to back up each of your claims.

Even if the employee becomes upset, you must remain calm, and you should stay in your seat. Avoid standing up quickly or moving suddenly. The only time you should ever touch the employee is to shake hands. Any other touching could be perceived as confrontational and may lead to physical violence.

After the exit interview, compose a report detailing the termination proceedings. File the report in the employee's personnel file. If the employee decides he or she wants to fight the termination, you will need the report to support your claims.

You should begin your search for a new employee as soon as possible. It will probably take several months before your new employee will reach the full level of productivity. There is the chance, of course, that following training, you will realize the employee is not going to work out after all.

There are no guarantees that a former employee is not going to take legal action to fight a termination. However, there are steps you can take to protect yourself and your business. First, you must be honest with your employee about his or her performance and why you are terminating him or her. Always be consistent in how you treat your employees, and be sure you always investigate any claims of harassment or discrimination.

Most importantly, you should document each chance you have given the employee to improve his or her performance before you have made the decision to terminate him or her. Unfortunately, if you fail to document the chances you have given the employee and he fights the termination, you might face repercussions. You do not need thorough notes, but you should ensure each note is dated and describes the problem and/or the progress the employee has made. Keep each note in the personnel file. Should you be faced with litigation, you will find that having these dated notes is extremely beneficial.

If you have other employees, understand that when they learn that a co-worker has been terminated, they, too, may experience insecurity in their positions. Some may even frown upon the situation, believing you are either unfair or harsh or both. Be prepared for the reaction from other employees. You may have to discuss the termination with the employees, and explain why the particular employee was let go.

The majority of the time, however, your employees will understand, as the problems are going to be obvious to everyone involved. Even when you discuss the termination with other employees, make sure you document the discussion and date it.

Tips for Motivating Your Employees

Even if you do not have employees now, chances are there will come a time when you will hire employees and need to keep them motivated. Hiring an employee or employees is a huge step in the growth of your Web-based business.

One of the keys to ensuring your employees provide you with the best of their abilities is to keep them motivated and excited about their jobs. If your employees will be home-based, you are already ahead of the game. According to Business Week, telecommuting is an effective way to ensure job satisfaction.

Even if your employees are onsite, there are plenty of other ways to keep them motivated and excited to work for you. First, you will likely find that one of the best and easiest ways to motivate your employees is to focus on the positive contributions they make to your business. Show them that you appreciate their hard work by running an Employee of the Month Contest, by taking them out to lunch, by offering them a day off during the week, or by giving them a small bonus.

Another key to your employees' happiness rests with effective communication. Think back to your days as an employee. You likely had ideas, frustrations, comments you wanted to share with your employer. Did you feel comfortable doing so? Welcome open communication and listen to your employees. They will feel valued which, in turn, will motivate them.

Offer your employees flexible schedules, if possible, and schedule regular performances reviews. Performance reviews allow you to offer positive reinforcement to your employees and reminders of what you expect from each of them.

If your employees work onsite, allow them to have fun with their workspace, as long as it does not go too far. Decorating work areas with photos of families, pets, friends, and other little trinkets can go a long way to ensuring your employees feel comfortable and happy — again, keys to improving their overall performance.

Finally, will your employees be able to advance in their positions as your Web-based business grows? Room for advancement is always an excellent motivator.

RESOURCES

Payment Options

PayPal – **www.paypal.com**

Google Checkout – **www.checkout.google.com**

2Checkout – **www.2checkout.com**

Affiliate Resources

Clickbank – **www.clickbank.com**

Commission Junction – **www.cj.com**

Better Business Bureau

Better Business Bureau – **www.bbb.org**

Better Business Bureau Online – **www.bbbonline.org**

National Chamber of Commerce

U.S. Chamber of Commerce – **www.uschamber.com**

Drop Shippers

Thomas Register – **www.thomasregister.com**

Worldwide Brands – **www.worldwidebrands.net**

Wholesale Dropshippers Directory – **www.wholesalecentral.com/Dropshippers.html**

World Wide Brands – **www.worldwidebrands.com**

Legal

Federal Trade Commission – **www.ftc.gov**

U.S. Trademark and Patent Office – **www.uspto.gov/main/trademarks.htm**

Internal Revenue Service (IRS) – **www.irs.gov**

Small Business Resources

SCORE – **www.score.org**

Small Business Administration (SBA) – **www.sba.gov**

Copyright Check

Copyscape – **www.copyscape.com**

Accounting software

Corel – **www.corel.com**

Microsoft – **www.microsoft.com**

Peachtree Accounting Software – **www.peachtree.com**

Bidding Sites

Elance – **www.elance.com**

Guru – **www.guru.com**

Rentacoder – **www.rentacoder.com**

Ifreelance – **www.ifreelance.com**

Domain Registrations

Domain Monger – **www.domainmonger.com**

Register.Com – **www.register.com**

Go Daddy – **www.godaddy.com**

Domain Bank, Inc. – **www.domainbank.net**

Yahoo Domains – **http://smallbusiness.yahoo.com/domains/**

Google Domains – **www.google.com**

Domain Lookup

Whois – **www.whois.net**

Domain Name Brokers

Buy Domains – **www.buydomains.com**

After Nic – **www.afternic.com**

Impressive Domains – **www.impressivedomains.com**

Web Site Names – **www.websitenames.com**

Web Site Broker – **www.websitebroker.com**

Blogging Resources

Blogger – **www.blogger.com**

Word Press – **www.wordpress.com**

Live Journal – **www.livejournal.com**

Blog Jet – **www.blogjet.com**

Blog.com – **www.blog.com**

Blog-City – **www.blog-city.com**

Blogster – **www.blogster.com**

Web Hosting

HostGator – **www.hostgator.com**

GoDaddy – **www.godaddy.com**

Ipower – **www.ipower.com**

Yahoo – **www.yahoo.com**

IX Web Hosting – **www.ixwebhosting.com**

BlueHost – **www.bluehost.com**

Lunarpages – **www.lunarpages.com**

Start Logic – **www.startlogic.com**

Easy CGI – **www.easycgi.com**

Globat – **www.globat.com**

Web Design Software

Dreamweaver – **www.adobe.com/products/dreamweaver/**

FrontPage – **www.adobe.com/products/dreamweaver/**

Web Studio 4.0 – **http://www.webstudio.com/**

Coffee Cup HTML Editor – **www.coffeecup.com/html-editor**

Adobe GoLive – **www.adobe.com/products/golive**

Popular Firewalls

Microsoft Windows Firewall – **www.microsoft.com/windowsxp/using/networking/security/winfirewall.mspx**

Norton Internet Security Personal Firewall – **www.symantec.com/home_homeoffice/products/overview.jsp?pcid=is&pvid=npf2006**

Check Point Zone Alarm – **www.zonelabs.com/store/content/home.jsp**

McAfee Personal Firewall – **www.mcafeestore.com/dr/sat3/ec_MAIN.**

**Entry10?V1=761606&PN=1&SP=10023&xid=49745&CUR=702&
DSP=&PGRP=0&ABCODE=&CACHE_ID=0**

AVG Internet Security – **www.grisoft.com**

Windows Live OneCare – **http://onecare.live.com/standard/en-us/
default.htm**

Spybot – **www.spybot.info/**

Web Site Security

VeriSign - **www.verisign.com**

TRUSTe - **www.truste.org**

Networking Resources

Ryze Business Networking – **www.ryze.com**

BNI International (The Business Referral Organization) – **www.bni.com**

Toastmasters – **www.toastmasters.org**

LeTip International – **www.letip.com**

The U.S. Chamber of Commerce – **www.uschamber.com**

The Minority Business Network – **www.mbnet.com**

The Entrepreneurs' Organization – **www.eonetwork.org**

International Federation of Small & Medium Enterprises – **www.ifosme.org**

Peer Sight – **www.peersightonline.com**

The Small Business Community Forums – **www.smallbusinessforums.org**

Podcasting Software

BlogMatrix Sparks – **www.blogmatrix.com**

ePodcast Creator – **www.industrialaudiosoftware.com/products/
epodcastcreator.html**

RecorderPro – **www.soniclear.com/ProductsRecorderPro.html**

Record For All – **www.recordforall.com**

CastBlaster – **www.castblaster.com**

Audacity – **audacity.sourceforge.net/download/**

Logo Design Resources

Logo Design Studio – **www.snapfiles.com/get/logodesignstudio.html**

Logo Creator – **www.thelogocreator.com**

Corporate Identity Creator – **www.cicreator.com**

AAA Logo (Logo Design Software – **www.aaa-logo.com**

Mix FX – Flash Logo Design – **www.mix-fx.com/flash-logos-design/ flashlogos.html**

Press Release Distribution

24-7 Press Release – **www.24-7pressrelease.com**

PR Newswire – **www.prnewswire.com**

PR.com – **www.pr.com/press-releases**

Market Wire – **www.marketwire.com**

I-Newswire – **www.i-newswire.com**

Business Wire – **home.businesswire.com/portal/site/home/index. jsp?front_door=true**

PR Web Direct – **www.prwebdirect.com**

E-mail Wire – **www.emailwire.com/cgi-bin/news/db.cgi?db=customer**

Article Directories

Ezine Articles – **http://ezinearticles.com**

Go Articles – **www.goarticles.com**

Article Dashboard – **www.articledashboard.com**

Article Pros – **www.articlepros.com**

Article Alley – **www.articlealley.com**

Add Articles – **www.add-articles.com**

Online Directories

Online Yellow Pages – **www.yp.com**

Superpages: Yellow Pages & White Pages – **www.superpages.com**

Jayde.com – **www.jayde.com**

Where2Go – **www.where2go.com**

Home Business Directory – **www.links4rank.com**

Business Week Business Directory – **http://businessweek.directorym.com/**

Biz Journals Directory – **www.bizjournalsdirectory.com/?source=96**

Search Engine Submission

Yahoo – **http://search.yahoo.com/info/submit.html**

Google – **www.google.com/addurl/**

MSN – **http://submitit.bcentral.com/msnsubmit.htm**

Exact Seek – **www.exactseek.com/add.html**

Alta Vista – **www.altavista.com/addurl/default**

AlltheWeb – **www.alltheweb.com/help/webmaster/submit_site**

Open Directory – **http://dmoz.org/add.html**

Netscape – **http://wp.netscape.com/escapes/search/addsite.html**

Add Me – **www.addme.com**

Web Traffic Analysis Tools

Stat Counter – **www.statcounter.com/**

Open Tracker – **www.opentracker.net/index.jsp**

One Stat – **www.onestat.com/**

Add Free Stats – **www.addfreestats.com/**

Benchmark Tracking – **www.benchmarktracking.com/**

ROI Tracking Pro – **www.roi-tracking-pro.com/**

BIBLIOGRAPHY

U.S. Department of Commerce Press Release: Quarterly Retail E-Commerce Sales 2nd Quarter 2006. **http://www.census.gov/mrts/www/data/html/06Q2.html**

Basic Bookkeeping Tips AllBusiness.com. 15 November 2004. **http://www. allbusiness.com/accounting/methods-standards/997-2.html**

BBB Tips on Putting Together a Budget Better Business Bureau. **http://www. bbb.org/alerts/article.asp?ID=648**

Business Plan: The Financial Management Plan SBA. **http://www.sba.gov/ gopher/Business-Development/Business-Initiatives-Education-Training/ Business-Plan/bp12.txt**

Edwards, Paul and Sara. *Work This Way – Obtaining a Resale License* Entrepreneur. June 2000. **http://findarticles.com/p/articles/mi_m0DTI/ is_6_28/ai_63192130**

Firing a Client National Federation of Independent Business. **http://www. nfib.com/object/3671521.html**

German, Kent. *The Top 10 Dot-Com Flops* CNET.com. **http://www.cnet. com/4520-11136_1-6278387-1.html**

Gilbert, Rona. *How Businesses Can Protect Themselves and Reduce Their Risk* Smart Business. December 2006. **http://www.sbnonline.com/National/ Article.aspx?CompanyID=83&Category=153&CID=10370**

Glasner, Joanna. *Why Webvan Drove Off a Cliff* WIRED. 10 July 2001. **http://www.wired.com/techbiz/media/news/2001/07/45098**

How Do I Set Shipping Rates? All Business.com http://www.allbusiness.com/ operatoins/shipping/1060-1.html

How to Price Your Products and Services Arkansas SBDC: Arkansas' Premier Business Assistance Program. http://asbdc.ualr.edu/bizfacts/1009.asp

IC3 – 2005 Internet Crime Report. National White Collar Crime Center and the Federal Bureau of Investigation. http://www.ic3.gov/media/ annualreport/2005_IC3Report.pdf

Inventor Resources United States Patent and Trademark Office. http://www. uspto.gov/web/offices/com/iip/patents.htm#CanAndCannotPatent

Insuring Your Home Business Nolo.com **www.nolo.com/article.cfm/ objectID/900932C5-C94D-47D1-AC154B36E81404B7/111/159/264/ART/**

Internal Revenue Service. **http://www.irs.gov/businesses/small/ article/0,,id=98240,00.html**

Is it Illegal to Not Get Paid for Job Training? Allbusiness.com **http://www. allbusiness.com/human-resources/careers-job-training/1131-1.html**

Kandler, David. *How to know what kind of online newsletter to publish* **http:// www.companynewsletters.com/electronic.htm**

Kivelan, Chris. *Choosing the Right Web Host* Entrepreneur.com 3 May 2006. **http://www.entrepreneur.com/ebusiness/gettingstarted/article163594.html**

Kobliski, Kathy J. *TV Ads: No Matter Who You're Trying to Reach, You'll Find Plenty of Opportunities on Network tTelevision.* Entrepreneur.com 17 January 2006. **http://www.entrepreneur.com/advertising/adsbytype/article83108.html**

Lisante, Joan E. *Worker's Compensation Insurance: Find out whether you need it and how to get it* Entrepreneur.com 20 April 2001. **http://www.entrepreneur.**

com/management/insurance/typesofinsurance/article39844.html

Loyalka, Michelle Dammon. *When Do You Really Need A Patent?* Business Week. 1 February 2006. http://www.businessweek.com/smallbiz/content/jan2006/sb20060131_731590.htm

Make Good Decisions SBA. http://www.sba.gov/smallbusinessplanner/manage/makedecisions/SERV_GOODDEC.html

McDowell, John. *Health Insurance Tax Deductions Help Entrepreneurs* SBA. 4 April 2006. http://www.sba.gov/advo/press/06-10.html

Microsoft Security Glossary. 19 December 2005. http://www.microsoft.com/security/glossary.mspx

Pricing Your Products U.S. Small Business Administration. http://www.sba.gov/library/pubs/fm-13.txt

Profit and Loss Statement SCORE. http://www.scoreknox.org/library/profit.htm

Schifferes, Steve. *Has the Dotcom Boom Returned?* BBC News. 10 October 2006. http://news.bbc.co.uk/2/hi/business/6036337.stm

Schnepper, Jeff. *The Ultimate Tax Shelter: Owning Your Own Business* http://articles.moneycentral.msn.com/Taxes/TaxShelters/TheUltimateTaxShelterYourOwnBusiness.aspx

Survive an Audit NOLO.com http://smallbusiness.yahoo.com/r-article-a-41100-m-2-sc-59-survive_an_audit-i

Taylor, Leslie. T*he Dotcom Bust? Not As Bad As You Think* FoxNews.com. http://www.foxnews.com/story/0,2933,234518,00.html

5 Tips for Taking Your Small Business Online SCORE. http://www.score.org/5_tips_eb_10.html

5 Tips for Developing Employees SCORE. 5 http://www.score.org/5_tips_tr_1.html

AUTHOR DEDICATION AND BIOGRAPHY

For my grandmother and grandfather and my mom and dad: Thank you for a lifetime of love, encouragement, and support. I love you.

Beth Williams is a full-time writer from Lexington, Virginia. In addition to a B.A. in Journalism and Communications from Point Park University, Beth holds a M.A. in Holocaust and Genocide Studies from The Richard Stockton College of New Jersey.

She is the founder and co-owner of Creative Inklings LC, a full-service writing firm that caters to both online and offline clients and can be found on the Web at **www.creativeinklings.org**. Beth has written hundreds of articles, e-books, audio scripts, reports, and other content for clients on dozens of topics ranging from business to travel. Additionally, she has written for several magazines, including those focusing on business.

Beth is currently taking her extensive writing credentials in a new direction, branching into internet marketing, offering private label rights (PLR) content for marketers, Webmasters, and other clients.

INDEX